OUR
NEED
OF LOVE

Dr. PAUL CHAUCHARD

OUR
NEED
OF LOVE

translated by UNA MORRISSY
foreword by HANS G. FURTH

P. J. KENEDY & SONS   NEW YORK

Our Need of Love is a translation of *Notre besoin d'amour,* first
published in 1965 by Editions
Salvator, Mulhouse and Paris.

COPYRIGHT © 1968 BY P. J. KENEDY & SONS

LIBRARY OF CONGRESS CATALOG CARD NUMBER 68–22877

PRINTED IN THE UNITED STATES OF AMERICA

Passages from the following works by Pierre Teilhard de Chardin have
been quoted in their authorized English translation:

The Divine Milieu. Copyright 1957 by Editions du Seuil, Paris. English
translation copyright © 1960 by William Collins Sons & Co., Ltd.,
London, and Harper & Row, Publishers, Inc., New York.

The Future of Man. Copyright 1959 by Editions du Seuil, Paris. English
translation by Norman Denny copyright © 1964 by William Collins Sons
& Co., Ltd., London, and Harper & Row, Publishers, Inc., New York.

Hymn of the Universe. Copyright © 1961 by Editions du Seuil, Paris.
English translation copyright © 1965 by William Collins Sons & Co., Ltd.,
London, and Harper & Row, Publishers, Inc., New York.

Reprinted by permission of the publisher.

Foreword

Teilhard de Chardin, a mystic and a scientist, has captured the imagination of this generation as hardly another religious savant during the past centuries. Whatever the motive behind his popularity, one cannot but consider the present interest in Teilhard's message as a hopeful sign in our present turbulent world. Teilhard's vision combines values that have been acclaimed each in its own right and frequently as opposed to each other: the material world of the scientist, the spiritual world of the religious, and the existential world of the creative seer.

5

In the present book, the work of a follower of that religious scientific poet, the author (and his excellent translator) center on the concept of love from a Teilhardian viewpoint. Chauchard's is the difficult task of applying Teilhard's vision—or better, of bringing it down to a more practical and rational level. This may not please some who prefer Teilhard's own poetic imagery, but it surely is necessary for the survival of that vision —and indeed for the implementation of the gospel mandate in a secularized and "hominized" world.

The points that Chauchard stresses are so beautiful and wholesome that some of his partial simplifications may be forgiven. By simplification I refer, for instance, to his formulation of a one-to-one correspondence between parts of the brain and human experience. He calls the brain the "organ" of love, with instinctual, rational, and personal love residing respectively in the primitive, cortical, and pre-frontal brain. I should hope that one can have a thoroughly biological view of man without having to localize each experience in special physiological regions.

The importance of Chauchard's thesis unquestionably lies in his attempt to counteract the evil of a contemporary conception of love that separates spiritual *agape* from physical *eros* by stressing one to the detriment of the other. He believes that this new view of love must make use of two convergent directions—"that of a complete science that is not content with a superficial knowledge of man, and that of a complete Christian faith that does not ignore the divine dimension of the earth." In this perspective the separate entities of our bourgeois experience, such as world and God, science and religion, solidarity and solitariness, instinct and reason, and, last but not least, intellect and love are seen as inseparable biological wholes, not as things that are to be brought together by some extrinsic determination, whether natural or supernatural.

Throughout the book one comes face to face with a radiant optimism and a therapeutic atmosphere that does not shrink from the stark realities of human life. If Teilhard's view has at times been misunderstood as a veiled pantheism, Chauchard wants to show that this view primarily proclaims the immanence of a transcendent God. He insists that transcendence without immanence is as harmful to a *complete* concept of God as is immanence without transcendence. If Christians have long accepted that "God is love," Chauchard following Teilhard's footsteps proposes that man is love, indeed the entire universe is love, from its primitive manifestation to its ultimate evolution.

Teilhard's voice, as interpreted by Chauchard, may not sound altogether convincing to all readers. Yet it is hard to see in what other directions man can look for the foundations on which to base the infinite value of the world and of the human task. We must be grateful to the author for presenting us with a splendid expression of such a conviction.

HANS G. FURTH

The Catholic University of America
Washington, D. C.

Contents

OUR
NEED
OF LOVE

CHAPTER 1

LOVING IS BELIEVING

An Introduction

WITH A SANE and optimistic realism that answers so well to the anxiety of the modern world—since indeed it is anxiety overcome—Teilhard de Chardin shows us mankind brought face to face with a choice between suicide and love. "We have only to believe," says Teilhard. "And the more threatening and irreducible reality appears, the more firmly and desperately must we believe. Then, little by little, we shall see the universal horror unbend, and then smile upon us, and then take us in its more than human arms. . ."

In the evening of his life the aged apostle John, then as always leaning upon his Master's breast, could repeat only, My little children, love one another as He has loved us.

What is this Christian love? First of all, we are required to believe. But after that, doesn't it seem to this world, with its passion for action, that all Christian love amounts to is resignation to suffering in this vale of tears in order to win the prize of heaven, where we shall all be clad in white and sing pious hymns? Technological modern man is both a conqueror and a constructor. Yet there are times when he can dwell only in despair on the uselessness of his labor, for all his effort will not prevent him from dying, will not prevent his species from disappearing, and will not prevent the world from coming to an end—perhaps through his own fault. Of what use is science fiction with its utopias of an *ersatz* immortality eternally renewed, or a stoicism that extols resignation, or the sense of brotherly involvement of a Camus who stakes the dignity of man on man's rejection of suicide: capitulation to the absurdity of nothingness?

Let us listen to Teilhard again. . . . "Because we have believed intensely and with pure hearts in the world, the world will open God's arms to us." And again: "In truth, I see the complete solution to the problem of happiness; I see it in the direction of a Christian humanism, or, if you prefer, in that of a superhuman Christianity, at whose heart every man will one day understand that it is possible for him, at every moment and in every situation, not only to serve (which is not enough) but also to cherish in everything (the most charming and beautiful as well as the most bitter and the most trivial) a universe filled with love in its evolution."

Apostle of a Sacred Heart now at last fully understood, Teilhard could only repeat tirelessly what had laid hold of him in his meditations at Verdun: There is no such thing as the world and God. Love is neither a duty nor a pleasure: it is the secret of our being, our essential element as beings created by the energy of love and created to build the world by the energy of love: *amorizators*. The whole evolutive creation that co-creative man achieves through his technical competence is an *amorizing* unification, one that proceeds from the many to the one, from the less loved, less lovable, the less loving to the more loved, the more lovable, the more loving who is God.

Blind world of men, you who excuse your inability to see God with the plea that the intellectuals have made Him invisible by destroying the childlike innocence of our hearts, you must find God again through His immanence in the heart of matter. The great mystery is that all objectively and scientifically love can be discovered as the secret of the world. In reflecting logically upon the love ascending to the heart of the world, one comes naturally to see in it the sign of God. But, without even going so far as that, the simple love at the heart of the world is enough to give us the power we need to live—that is, to engage enthusiastically in the *process of amorization*.

What the wonderful modern world is missing is an understanding of love. And so it is turning into a preserve of despair and of the absurd. It is a world whose songs continually speak of love, and yet it is dying for lack of love. And what is love? The repose of the soldier, of the scholar, of the scientist, in the arms of a compliant woman? Teilhard it is who invites us to focus our eyes clearly and to look upon the horrifying loss of energy and of the essential energy of love resulting from a life-style in which erotism is no more than a sensual automatism, love a cheap sentimentality, and where that essential value, sex, has turned into a social scourge. And what have we made of woman, witness to authentic love? We either ignore the "dangerous" sex altogether or we debase woman by misunderstanding her.

According to Teilhard, "To master passion in order to make it serve the spirit would be, on biological evidence, a condition for progress. Therefore, despite our incredulity, the world will sooner or later take this step. For all that is truest comes to pass; and everything happens for the best in the end. Every day, from the air, the winds, the tides, the force of gravity, we shall harness [Teilhard says for God, but it is primarily for man, because all that is for man is for God] the energies of love. And then, for the second time in the history of the world, man will have discovered Fire.'

Very well then, some will say, find and make use of love—but it is going to involve risk. So does the atomic adventure, which we would not dream of preventing but only of utilizing in the service of good, and with a prudence whose true name is *calculated risk.* But while the atomic adventure followed upon scientific progress that made experimentation permissible for us, the adventure of love is so basic to our destiny that prohibitions and barriers can keep only the very rare individual—and then at the risk of serious disturbance—from accepting life, from embarking upon it. And still we make unfortunate and destructive "adventures" out of this supreme adventure, and lose our hearts on them. So, since it is impossible to avoid the risk, let us give it its true meaning by understanding love.

"I shall take good care [says Teilhard] not to deny the destructive or disintegrative potentialities of passion. I shall even agree, in this regard, that outside the reproductive function, men have used love chiefly to become corrupted and decadent. But what do such excesses prove? Because flames can consume and electricity blast, are we to stop making use of them for our own benefit? Woman is the most redoubtable of the forces of matter. That is obvious. 'Therefore she must be avoided,' say the moralists. 'Therefore she must be understood and included,' say I. In all the gifts of the Reality (physical, affective, intellectual) 'danger' is an indication of power. . . . The more dangerous a thing is, the more its conquest is ordained by Life.

From this conviction has emerged the modern world. From this also must our religion be reborn.

This is a matter of control and correct use. Yet the unconcern of the activist and the technocrat means that through ignorance he is the one controlled and used rather than the one who controls and uses correctly. We are being borne along by the ever-quickening current we call *progress*. But it is not only conservative thinkers or obstinate worshipers of the past who realize that this is not necessarily an authentic human progress. These ills of civilization are symbolic—the therapeutic ills we are succumbing to in greater and greater degree, stuffed as we are with pills so as to keep going despite our exhaustion. Won't we all become mad in a mad world, dreaming of a wonderful psychiatric clinic where the mad will be sheltered and cured?

Yet if the world is mad it is largely our fault. Our crime lies not so much in willing evil, in being consciously wicked, as in our ignorance, our imprudence, our negligence, our stupidity, our lack of foresight.

We grow indignant on the subject of the destructive tendencies of the "beatniks," that universal brotherhood of West and East, because they are not like us. We should do better to admit that they are simply more logical and less hypocritical than we are. They obey no laws or customs, and quite openly they do wrong. We do it only in secret, or when there is no danger, or when it is within the law. It is true, we are not going to murder, vandalize, or rob openly, but we are still contriving to murder, vandalize, and rob legally, in a genteel way.

Teenagers are heedless and irresponsible, as are, of course, the beatniks and hippies; but let us recognize that we are quite as heedless and irresponsible as they. Then let us face up to the things we do with a perfectly good conscience, to this world, hideous with poverty, war, and hunger, which we are about to hand over to the young; and let us admit that we are beatniks,

stupidity — lack of good

and that the world is beatnik, too—that is, evil in general, through sheer stupidity. Indeed, the psychologists have confirmed this by passing on the beatnik "battle-cry" to us.[1] If there are beatniks it is the fault of this world, a world depraved through stupidity, a world where children cannot help growing up like savages if they are deprived of love.

These teenagers in revolt are more sincere than we are. It was we who taught them that the world was absurd, and the incoherence of our actions has never failed to confirm this in their judgment. Under these conditions they reject the conformism of honorable and useless work, and expend their energies by throwing themselves into a frenzy of destructive living, finding comfort in this inhuman world in the collective memory of the gang and in community action performed in friendship—everything that the normal world, individualistic or totalitarian, has been unable to give them. Their sole mistake is that basically they put too much faith in the opinion of adults. For these preachers of a virtue that they do not practice have brought young people around to thinking that if they have made an absurd world it is because everything is in fact absurd. So, instead of helping to extend it further into absurdity, why not reject these ineffectual adults and resolve to do better than they have done, to do all the wonderful things that are possible tomorrow if we so wish it?

That, alas, would be Utopia. For to make such a wise decision they would have to be more adult than those same false mentors who have prevented them from genuinely maturing, from having the strength and ability to root out the rich and

---

1. See *Cri d'appel d'un blouson-noir. Un document authentique* (Paris, 1962). In the face of the absurdity of the world made by the adults, the beatniks dissolved themselves in a destructive violence. Today the hippies prefer to escape from themselves by non-violence and psychedelic "trips": two inverse forms of disengagement that lead to nothing but self-destruction in the course of destroying the world a little more.

powerful from the enervating egoism in which they are entrenched.

Is there no escape from the situation? Are we doomed to
witness the destruction of the world through the utter stupidity
of human beings in the foolish conflict between amoralism and
moralism (for one is as irresponsible as the other) : the destructive automatisms of vice and alternatively of false, legalistic,
pharisaical virtue?

A pessimism such as this, which keeps telling us that everything is going from bad to worse in the worst of worlds is just as
false and pernicious as the fatuous optimism that says that
everything is of necessity becoming better in the best of worlds.
The world was made to become better, but only on condition
that men desire and find out what constitutes the best. It is
through ignorance that without wishing to or even realizing it
we are making a bad job of it. We know how to operate and
maintain our machines, but we do not know—for we are under
the impression that this comes about of its own accord—how to
operate our human machine. Yet the technique of being
human, which is indispensable to us if we are to be happy in a
happy world, is very simply the technique of learning to love:
to love ourselves, to love other people, to be lovable, and to
understand that it is our business to build with love a lovable
world.

Who will teach us this? The preceptors of the modern world,
in their revolt against moralistic oppression, lay great stress
upon the values of involvement, of freedom, of action. Here
they are right enough, but they show themselves to be dangerously destructive when they offer nothing to orientate our involvement toward it. It is the good that must be sought in
freedom. There can be no humanity where there is no freedom;
but freedom is human only when it is made to serve an objective good: this is an absolute reference that must be looked for
in every situation. The goal of action is not the satisfaction of

my whims, the sensual gorging on all the "foods of the earth" in the stupid refusal to distinguish between food and poison, between the neurotic and the normal (Gide) , in the expression of the will to power of the superman—which, of course, I am.

Jean Paul Sartre is certainly not responsible for all the excesses of the Existentialist cult, but he is responsible for the destructive scourge itself, which, by rejecting man, has made him the slave of the technocrats. . . . Isn't it paradoxical to fight courageously for social justice—that is to say, for the elevation of man—when one has stated that man does not exist? Nothing is more ambiguous or paradoxical than the little work "Extentialism Is a Humanism," since, from the tenable affirmation that man does not exist and that there are only men, it goes on to ignore the fact that man exists in what men have in common; and then proclaims a freedom of total choice through systematically eliminating certain choices.

Man does not possess a human nature, we are told. Very well; but human nature is there in him as an aptitude, a vocation, a duty. Man is nothing other than what he makes himself. Agreed; but what he makes himself is truth or falsehood, self-fulfillment or self-destruction. It is simply ambiguous to declare: "To choose to be this or that is to affirm at the same time the value of what we choose, for we can never choose evil; what we choose is always the good, and nothing can be good for us without being good for all."

How tempting this total liberty is. And yet, while appearing to lay the foundation of a value, it is really suppressing it. For why doesn't Sartre offer us the freedom to be fascists? Why, in the example of the young man who is hesitating between the two goods of remaining with his mother or going to fight with the Résistance, does he not speak of those two other choices, namely, killing his mother or serving the Nazis? That indeed would be a fully Existentialist liberty.

It is the tragedy of the spirit of the Left that it fights courageously for the good while contending that good does not exist. It is the error of the spirit of the Right that it defends an adventitious good that is actually an entrenched injustice instead of laboring to bring the true good into being. We may understand why men of today, faced as they are with the impossibility of political-humanistic involvement, have lost interest in an absurd world; yet it is absurd only because of the ignorance and incoherence of its preceptors and leaders.

We need a morality that will hold out a *value common to all men,* for we are divided between religious systems of morality limiting our freedom of action and secular moral codes that state precisely what to do and destroy reason into the bargain. Thus, if God does not exist everything is permissible: this is the outlook of a great many believers and unbelievers alike. And a mistaken outlook it is. It is as though God commanded us not to jump from a fifth-floor window—an order that the unbeliever, who does not accept Creation, may refuse. Of course, unbelievers and believers have the wisdom not to jump for the selfsame reason—that they know they would kill themselves. The unbelievers will be satisfied to talk about the fall of bodies and gravitation, while the believers will see in the interdict a natural law leading them to God, who is responsible for the harmony of the universe.

This is valid in every area; for we must discover a *natural* human morality, a consensus on right conduct in view of what we are. And it is in effect in the name of such a morality that the Catholic Church counsels the world through the voices—all in agreement—of Pius XII, John XXIII, and Paul VI. But if this natural morality is put forward by the moralist in its full supernatural justification, it is not readily credited with being natural and valid for everyone.

The most urgent task today, therefore, is to develop a *scientific, normative knowledge of human nature.* But if we are to accomplish this we shall have to scrap the assumption that science, which speaks in the indicative, offers us nothing that we could convert into an imperative.[2]

And so it must be from the objective standpoint of science—but a *complete* science—that we are going to seek what love is and why it is our essential need. But isn't it unscientific to talk of love? It is just because of this preconceived notion that we misunderstand the nature of love. The day will come when the principal teaching given to men will be this science of love, this prospective *agapologia* in the service of true human progress—and not simply the science of love, but a technique of *amorization*.

In order to achieve this "common front for human advancement" posited by Teilhard as a political base, it is necessary that atheists, recognizing the objective realities of love, be tempted to climb up from this natural love to the God who sustains it; but it is just as necessary for Christians to bring love back down on earth, and to stop being, as they too often are, people who show no love despite their claim to love "in God." [3]

A candid look at love requires that we make use of the two convergent points of view—that of a complete science that is not content with a superficial knowledge of man, and that of a complete Christian faith that does not ignore the divine dimension of the earth.

What about the impulse to "live dangerously" by risking everything in the wonderful adventure of our freedom? There will be room for this, too. But it must not be with the destructive force of desperation. What we have to conquer is ourselves: we must make a success of ourselves, we must realize ourselves,

2. The author has developed this topic in other works, such as *L'homme normal* (Paris, 1963); *La morale du cerveau* (Paris, 1962).

3. See the author's *La science, détruit-elle la religion?* (Paris, 1958), trans. by S. J. Tester as *Science and Religion* (New York, 1962); *La vocation chrétienne de l'homme d'aujourd'hui* (1965); and *La Pensée scientifique de Teilhard* (1965).

extend ourselves in the authenticity of our individual vocation—which is first of all a human vocation. And all this we
must do not independently but interdependently, helping others to realize themselves freely. We must be passionate, but the
only passion worth having is that for the optimum, the golden
mean. This is not the safe situation of the non-aligned, settled
comfortably in his armchair, but the road along the ridge, a
road that climbs sharply and dangerously between two precipices
toward the light at the summit.

The thing is not to listen to the messengers of despair and the
absurd. The world has a meaning, human life has a meaning.
We are not shackled to a moral code that would prevent us
from living; we are not locked up in a technocratic technology.
We have a world to build well, and that world is first and
foremost ourselves. Everything is possible if we believe in it—
enough, that is, to involve ourselves with our whole hearts.

Is it possible that in this overpopulated world there can be so
huge a harvest and yet a shortage of laborers? Is it possible that
people can actually be bored in so small a world, while everything has still to be done?

We should listen to the message, too often ignored, of Pierre
Termier (1859–1930), a distinguished geologist who flourished
long before Teilhard and, like Teilhard, believed passionately
in the "glory of the earth" and the vocation of the scientist.
"What shall we say to the passers-by?" he asks.—"That life is
made for enjoyment? that the essential thing is to be stronger
than one's neighbors, cleverer, better armed, richer? that in this
short voyage of life nothing is intelligible, absolutely nothing;
and that we are handed over as worthless playthings to a hostile
Nature?"

No, he replies. "We shall say something quite different. We
shall cry out to each man: Try to understand, try to know, and
at all events, love; seek to rise above yourself, in spite of
weights holding you down; climb into comprehension, into

knowledge and into love; choose, if you have the choice, poverty to wealth because wealth will weigh you down whereas poverty will lighten you; choose readily 'to be the lamb which gives its fleece'; do not fear sadness nor suffering nor death, for all three are the instruments of redemption, and you should feel, in your very depths, that you need to redeem yourself and to contribute to the redemption of your fellow men; consider yourself happy to serve . . . ; open your eyes to the beauty of the world and your soul to its mystery; and when you have understood, explain it to your fellow men; spread out your soul!"

Loving is believing.

CHAPTER 2

LOVE AND THE INTELLECT

Feeling, Reason, Love

HAS LOVE A PHYSICAL ORGAN that could be studied objectively by the biologist?

Since love, as the dictionary tells us, is "an impulse of the heart toward someone or something that attracts it," our attention is focused upon the organ that indicates our passions by its accelerations and sudden palpitations. But however important may be the amatory manifestations of this hollow muscle, we needn't fall into the crude materialism of identifying the headquarters of the circulation of the blood with the seat of the emotions. For although, if one were to judge by the carvings on unknown numbers of trees, the heart is the symbol of lovers, love is nonetheless a spiritual force.

One need not be a student of Freud to counter that by saying that the spiritual love prompting us to ask for someone's "hand" is in reality an urge to seek genital satisfaction. Shouldn't we honestly admit, then, that the "heart" is not in the breast but is to be identified with the genital organs? Modern psychology would probably go along with this, since it sees in our emotional life only *eros*, the *libido*, and their sublimation, and gives an erotic interpretation to both the oral and the anal stages of the nursling.

Whatever its importance, the fact is that sex, like the heart organ or any muscle that enables us to act, is merely an agent of activity. What really counts is the organ of control, responsible for both knowledge and activity—namely, the brain.

The brain the organ of love? Gruesome thought, one may say. Are we trying to say that love should be "cerebral," intellectual, subject to dispassionate reason, and, if not indeed prosaic, at any rate lacking in all spontaneity and poetry, a physical exercise? Well, is it possible to have spontaneity and poetry without the brain, as in the case of someone in a coma? To consider the role of the intellect in this matter of love is not only the way to study love objectively and scientifically, it is the only possible way of restoring to love its lost unity.

On the one hand we have ideal spiritual love—platonic, of course, and shorn of the flesh and the emotions; and on the other, erotic, carnal, and sentimental love. The nun endeavors to love God without loving Him with her woman's heart, and the wife consents to the necessity for "nature" in sexual intercourse, provided that her husband has been able to prepare her in a spiritual and emotive context: he knows that it would not be seemly to go as far with her as his desire would suggest to him. Eros or agape? Here we have an artificial division, one that the psychophysiology of love will spare us.

The intellect is the organ both conditioning the spirituality and regulating the emotional reaction that permits sensuality and its control and directs the activity of our sexual organs. To observe it in love is to understand that love is complete only if eros is not deprived of its agape, which is there to control it. This is the ambiguousness of erotism, which drops in value without the spiritual element; and the ambiguousness of spiritual love, which is not love unless it is physical.

But the brain is not merely the intellectual organ of cool reason. Our real "heart" is also the brain. To cerebralize the heart is not to deny it but to understand it.

In every age philosophers have discussed the question whether the heart is inferior to or superior to reason. In every age men and women have argued it. The woman claims the primacy of the heart, the supreme dimension of her personality by means of which she desires intuitively and irrationally to rule the world. The man, intellectual and technician, measures and calculates rationally without taking the emotions into account; he is accused of being "heartless," appearing to have a heart only at the dictate of his sexual needs.

Should one build the world out of a technical manual or from the promptings of the heart? Should one take refuge from the technical manual in the promptings of the heart? Should the woman who earns her living (that is, professionally, outside the home, since the mother who is only a mother has no profession!) be a split personality, a masculine person who thinks like a man but remains a woman, a female object of desire? How can this ambivalence requiring her to be both man and woman allow her to keep her balance?

It is the neurophysiology of love that provides us with the solution to that problem. *We have three layers in our brain.*

There is an elementary brain, the lower or primitive, anatomically known as rhinencephalon and hypothalamus. This is our heart in the sense of being the seat of instinctual emotions; in the sense that it tends to free the urges of the heart. To stop at this level (a feminine temptation) is to deny all our intellectual and rational superiority, for undoubtedly this heart is inferior to reason. It controls the palpitations of the heart-organ and the genital motions; its work is with the blood, hormones, and secretions.

Much more human than this primitive brain (which is purely animal), is the upper brain overlying it with all the richness of its complex nervous system. This whole cerebral outer layer is the *neotic* brain: the seat of sensory percepts and motory controls, responsible for the sensations and volitions that may be likened to our machine for thinking and reasoning with words. This is the brain that also gives us the knowledge of our own ego as distinct from the body and from the external world; that allows us also to learn to feel and to act, and to acquire new reactions and habits. The masculine judgment quite rightly prizes the brain of the intellectual and of the thinking technician above the lower brain.

But we do not have to be split personalities on this account, giving way successively to the very different activities of these two brains. The heart is human only if it is controlled by reason, but reason is human only if it is impassioned about what is rational. For a man deprived of emotion, or who has room for emotion only at certain moments, is neither normal nor complete. It is a pity that men and women should not be willing to synthesize their right intuitions by rejecting both the sentimentalist and the rationalist temptations.

Neurophysiology comes to our help here by showing us that the noetic brain is not made for supreme control any more than is the lower brain. Like the "sentimentalist," the intellectual paradoxically uses his brain very badly, and thus prejudices us against the "cerebral" person, though in reality his "cerebral" behavior is deprived of its principal function. Above these two afore-mentioned brains there is a third brain, and this one is the most specifically human, for it is developed in the succession of monkeys and prehumans, but reaches its full development only in man himself—*Homo sapiens,* regarded since ancient times as Cro-Magnon Man. It is the *prefrontal* brain, which gives man his forehead.

Progress in our knowledge of the functions of this region has come to us from pathology. The bilateral destruction of this region by a tumor or an accident changes the patient into an indifferent person, without care or responsibility, and alternating between a lack of feeling and a violent, uncontrollable emotionalism; he is like a child. His power of attention has diminished; he seems to lack memory; above all, he takes no part or interest in anything. The emotional disturbances in mental pathology (manic excitement or manic depression) may be lessened by the removal of the prefrontal brain (lobotomy). The patient is cured of his mental disease, but at the price of grave mutilation of the most human portion of his brain. Although cured, he is not normal and is often in misery on that account. We can only rejoice in the decline of this therapy, thanks to the emergence of pharmaceutical treatment of mental states. Observation of those who have been subjected to prefrontal lobotomy has taught us a great deal about the functions of this highest or noble brain. So too has observation of animals, dogs or monkeys who have had this region—inadequate in their case anyway—either completely removed by surgery or functionally disturbed by the passage of an electric current through it.

The complex supplementary circuits of our prefrontal brain serve neither sensory or motor ends directly; nor are they involved in emotional expression, in thought or intelligence. But in these circuits there is incarnated what might be called the "fine point of our soul," which we wrongly consider to be purely spiritual. There is nothing angelic in us, and everything in our being here below flows from the body. This fine point of our soul is the free and responsible dimension of our personality. It is capable of reflection as well as anxiety about the future, which it endeavors to foresee by using the experience of a past that is its history as presented by memory. If we, unlike the animal, can place ourselves above or outside present actions in order to assess and choose a line of conduct, we owe this physiologically to our prefrontal.

In our noetic brain we have the machinery for sensation and for action, while the cerebral image of the ego is the machine for willing. Simply adjusting the juxtaposition of these two machines gives the animal a certain openness for action that is non-reflective consciousness. The accomplishment of the "step of reflection" on the part of man is due to the power of associating the cerebral ego from outside the noetic brain, with the mechanics of execution, in order to give him the *physiological direction,* the power to arouse and to control. It is due to our prefrontal brain that we have our voluntary self-control. Thus the will appears not as a purely spiritual power that succeeds only in mortifying without correcting a rebellious flesh; it is rather the correct utilization of the prefrontal brain for control and coordination of the lower regions of the brain. Obviously then, man is not made as a machine for speaking, thinking, and acting in virtue of habits or whims. He is made for deciding what is fitting, for devising desirable ways of behavior.

The prefrontal is the brain of involvement. Reflection not only makes us decide what is suitable for us. It gives us the taste, the enthusiasm for what we choose. It does not give us merely a barren notional knowledge, but makes us assent with our whole hearts to what we know. And this is what would appear to be the full significance of the prefrontal. Its real name is the brain of the heart, the organ of love. But this no

longer refers to the emotions, or to the elemental sentimental-
ism or erotism of the lower brain: it carries the full human
meaning of the words used. To let oneself be carried away by
feelings or passion, or at the other extreme to reject all emotion, is to behave incompletely, and therefore inhumanly. Authentic reason, authentic human intelligence, the really "cerebral" approach, includes an emotional dimension, an aspect of
passion, but a passion wisely, lucidly, voluntarily controlled;
not a spurious, blinding passion, but the involvement of the
whole being in an enthusiasm through which our knowledge is
personalized, becomes a faith that is not inferior to our knowledge but in fact goes far beyond it. Thus belief is not reserved
to an act of religious faith. It concerns our whole life, whether
or not we are believers in the religious sense.

This is the way a total neurophysiology, when asked how the
brain enables us to act, takes us away from the debate about the
heart and reason in favor of understanding the *natural temptations* to denaturalization that lay in a merely partial grasp of
the truth by the masculine rationalist spirit and the feminine
sentimentalist spirit. We must act rationally, but we must passionately love this rationality. Our lives are not split between
significant activity based on reason on the one hand, and an
emotive *détente* on the other. The heart must always be in
command—but a heart that is no longer the mindless reflection
of its own emotional "hang-ups."

But neurophysiology has a message considerably more important still for the conduct of our lives. It is not enough to know
how we are made in order to act correctly. We must *learn it*.
Now, we are unaware of the genuine need to learn. We think
that it is all a matter of acquiring theoretical knowledge, or
techniques or moral rules. Our brains must be furnished indeed. But the important thing is not a head well filled but a
head well made. Now, a well-made human head does not depend simply on cerebral growth, which would automatically

make us normal when allied to good heredity and an environment conducive to growth. We must learn also to use this
complex machine correctly. We must learn not only what has to
be done but how to do it; we must learn to reflect, to will, to
control ourselves; we must learn to become involved, to become
impassioned; we must learn to believe.

This liberating machine does not make us automatically
free. To be free it is essential first of all to respect the physical
conditions governing our liberty—i.e., that we are to reflect
before acting and be capable of self-mastery, for if we cannot do
these things we are no more than automata of the lower emotive and noetic brains, and are making no use of the higher
prefrontal brain. Yet unfortunately we usually behave this way,
acting through impulse or conformity. Scientist J. Rostand is
perfectly logical when he casts doubt on our freedom. Not that
we have no natural disposition for freedom, only that we have
not learned how to use it. We do not reflect—and reflection is
the condition of liberty. This does not mean that we must
repress all impulses and habits, rather that we accept only those
that are good, those we may love passionately.

Those that are good. . . . Here is the second condition of our
liberty. Perfect, divine liberty can want only what is good. Our
human liberty is the power to do anything. Sartre is right there.
But he is wrong in thinking that this is because there is neither
good nor evil. There are two ways of doing the wrong thing.
One way is to act without reflection, and the other is to be
mistaken in one's reflection and to involve oneself in evil, not
necessarily in a clear choice of evil as such (which of course is
sin), but to choose evil in the mistake of imagining it to be for
our good. Now, our cerebral liberating machine is so made that
we can be free only if we involve ourselves in the area of some
good, and this is an objective human value that it is our duty to
discover.

It is not possible, from a cerebral standpoint, for man to

remain human and still gorge on all the foods of the earth. We must distrust the automatisms of our emotive and noetic brains. They are for our use, and it is convenient to let them work without always being forced to reflect; but one can do this only if one has acquired good habits. To indulge imprudently in one's whims, in sensuality, in aggressiveness, in conformity, amounts, in fact, to alienating one's liberty and losing all spontaneity. What we cherish as the spontaneity of freedom is generally the worst form of slavery to the impulses of the flesh and of the unconscious. The automaton of sensuality, of aggressiveness, and of conformity is a matter of man's no longer behaving as a man governed by his superior brain, and he becomes capable of the worst horrors.

But there is something still worse, and that is the deliberate choice of sensuality, aggressiveness, conformity simply because circumstances are favorable or there is good reason for the choice. The neuropath will give way without conscious motive to rape, or to aggressions in a fit of rage. He believes himself normal if he gives way only for good reason—as, for instance, because he is with a woman who is agreeable; or he must punish wrongdoing; or he has joined a social group, a party he believes in completely. One cannot indulge oneself even for good cause; our sensuality, our aggressiveness, our conformity are hazardous slopes of corruption, and very easy to slither down.

There is no normal sexuality without sensual control; the danger of just anger is that it might lead us to go beyond just limits; the drawback to blind obedience is that it can transform us into a lot of sheep, the prey to the herd instinct or to the hypnotism of the leader. This is not to say that all sensuality, all anger, all conformity are bad; but that it is vitally important to retain the just balance and to ignore neither the prefrontal control (which cannot be by-passed for more than a moment without its activity's becoming impossible to recover) nor the necessity for the noetic and the emotional brains to use their habits and impulses, but controlled and directed to the service of good.

It is necessary to bring the will into play at all times. But one cannot use the will for good except by willing what is good, and to will what is good presupposes the habit of willing the good. What is more, it demands that we will good not because of anxiety or scruples, but in relaxed and truly spontaneous fashion, with the ease of the professional athlete who has the air of succeeding without effort, because he is in training and is completely master of his own body.

The step of reflection, the start to any sane and enthusiastic involvement in good, was not given to man to improve his behavior in certain specific circumstances. Man is not only capable of reflection; *he is obliged to reflect, for he is made for it.* It may tire us always to bring the will into play, for we have not learned to use it effortlessly. So we like to think that it is not always necessary. Don't we have good instincts, like the animals? We incline to think that it is very pleasant to let loose the animal in us from time to time, all the more so since we have learned that it is dangerous to curb it excessively. This in general is what is meant by being spontaneous. The unfortunate thing is that however desirable it may seem to him, it is an utter impossibility for a man to conduct himself in animal fashion, for the obvious reason that he is not in fact an animal.

The animal is an automaton of the lower or instinctual brain; that is to say, his body causes him to do automatically whatever is necessary to feed himself or otherwise satisfy his needs according to the requirements and habits of his species, in conformity with his nature and his sexuality. The smooth operation of the hive or termitary does not depend upon the authority of a king or queen and the obedience of his or her subjects. There is no need to invoke a mysterious "spirit of the hive." Today we know something of the social reflexes that are released through interactions between individuals and regulate the harmony; there are "social hormones." But we may not conclude from this that the animal is a machine. Above the primitive brain's instinctual automatisms, which are always affective—that is, the good attracts and is pleasant, while the bad repels and is unpleasant—the higher brain allows of an improvement of behavior through the acquisition of habits, a rudimentary awareness of needs, a certain degree of deliberate control. Such improvement is the more noticeable according as the brain is more developed; yet it is not necessary for ensuring the basic functions of life.

In the case of man, however, we cross a threshold that involves a real difference of psychobiological nature. The higher brain is not only considerably more developed with the emergence of the prefrontal, it has become *necessary;* whereas the primitive brain, accustomed to function under its direction, is reduced in potentiality. *In the animal sense, man has no instincts.* His primitive brain is the source of needs but it no longer deploys the automatisms to satisfy them correctly. As the result of the superiority of his brain, man must learn to recognize his needs and to satisfy them deliberately and correctly, whence arises a grave risk of his making mistakes. This is the ambiguity of our superiority, and unless we know how to make use of it we may find ourselves inferior to animals.

What sort of thing, then, is this spontaneity through which we choose to act like animals? Actually it is a serious dehumanization, and it sinks far below the animals. We are not obeying good instincts, for we no longer have them; what we are assuming to be proper, unerring, uncoercible instinct is in reality nothing but habit: the manner we have absorbed from our environment of eating, or of exercising our sexuality, or whatever. It is merely a matter of social conformity; and, unlike instinct, it may involve prejudice, error, or bad habit. It is pretty hard for an animal, guided as he is by instinct, to become denaturalized. It is, on the contrary, easy for man, for man does not associate his liberty with his nature. In fact his liberty consists in finding, by means of reflection, whatever is natural in the human sense—that is to say, what is good, what is in conformity with the real needs and the real potentialities of the organism.

The animal lives healthily by automatism; man has to resort to a knowledge of hygiene. A complete psychosomatic hygiene of the brain and behavior rises eventually to the level of morality, and constitutes the biological aspect. Yet this should not be simply a matter of knowledge and of intellectual constraint for man. He should involve himself in this hygiene with eagerness and enthusiasm, once he has seen it as the actual law of his development and self-realization. The tragedy of man is that he can devote himself to mistaken needs and bad habits, and can adjust to them with an apparent satisfaction that people think is real happiness. Real happiness lies in thoughtful discovery and deliberate satisfaction of true needs through the full use of the brain. It does not lie in the rejection of new needs or new ways of satisfying them, but in the appreciation of what is good.

The Degrees of Love

We can be more explicit about the love at the heart of our beings, now that we have some knowledge of its organ.

The whole significance of this power of love, which the full use of our brain allows us, lies not in its power to love a person or a thing considered as an object to a certain extent outside of, though of concern to, ourselves, but in the fact that *we are beings of love,* that love forms part of our constitution. The brain's function is only to provide the power to make the love that is our being a better and more intensive love, a love achieving our unity and ensuring the standard of our relations to beings and things. This is to be a person.

Love is present at the biological origin of our existence; this is not simply the love of our father and mother for one another but at a more elementary level the *attraction,* analyzable in chemotaxes that the ovule exercises on the spermatozoa. There is no question here, of course, of attributing human love to the sexual cells, but of recognizing within an analogical perspective that it is the same energy presiding at the attraction of the elements, whatever may be the value of those elements. Atoms, molecules, cells, animals, human beings—all attract or repel one another in an affinity or a repulsion has an affective value and, in the broad sense of the word, can be called love. In the full sense of the word, of course, love exists only in man, who is capable of attractions and repulsions that are conscious and reflective. The human brain is required here. But this human love would not exist, as Teilhard saw so well, if it were not a general property of the material universe. A universe that is not a static cosmos but a *dynamism of cosmogenesis* is an *affective universe whose secret is love.* This love gives it complexity and unity and leads it toward more and more elaborate syntheses and organizations, from the multiple to the one.

From such a viewpoint, where the levels of organization of existing matter are the evidence of a long history of evolutionary progress in which the simple preceded the complex, it is possible to distinguish the *levels of love* in order to avoid anthropomorphic confusions;[1] while of course we make no such erroneous classification as to describe as pre-emotional and *pre*-love the inanimate interattractions that are still not psychologically ascribable to the emotions or to love. At the level of life, cells in which individuality is stronger and there is beginning to be manifested a unified psychism whose direction is

---

1. There is more on this topic in the author's *Teilhard. Temoin de l'amour* (Paris, 1962); translated by Marie Chêne as *Teilhard de Chardin on Love and Suffering* (New York, 1966).—*Ed.*

already in an elementary manner conscious (cellular consciousness or bio-consciousness), one may speak of the start of an individual assumption of affectivity in the psychic behavior: this is an automatism of *bio-love*.

Such bio-love is at the origin of the cellular union in conception and may already be classed as human, since it unites two human cells by virtue of their chemical nature. It must be understood, of course, that a human bio-love is not a reflective human love.

Once the ovum, the origin of the new individual, is fully formed it is going to display a prodigious dynamism of growth, consisting in an intense assimilation that leads it to divide into multiple cells. These latter cells, instead of dividing, remain united. And here again is revealed the love energy that shows itself in bio-love. In its unconscious automatisms the ovum loves itself—that is to say, it seeks what is necessary to it and if possible it rejects whatever does not suit it. Modern researches into unicellular activity have clearly shown a protoaffectivity expressing itself in conduct of choice, of preference. (See G. Viaud's *Les Tropismes* [Paris, 1951] on this point.) Even at this level the living thing is not a machine. But the sister cells resulting from the division of the ovum have an unconscious need of one another which physicochemistry will one day explain in its mechanisms—but this will not preclude seeing in it a protoaffective attraction also belonging within the framework of bio-love. The law "Thou shalt love thy neighbor as thyself" presides over the constituent automatisms of our organism, made up of cells not independent but interdependent, and manifesting their instinct for preservation by combining in order to survive. The mistake would be to see all this from an anthropomorphic standpoint, but it would also be a mistake to deny the analogy.

What of the higher organism, our body, which will develop from the ovum? It is a machine for surviving with more freedom under unfavorable conditions. A cell cannot thrive except in a liquid milieu; but within our organism cells live in an internal liquid milieu and the individual can still lead a life in the open air. We know how our cells form a true society with its own specializations, each owing its life to the others and placing its own life at the service of the others. This is well illustrated by the fable of the legs and the stomach. Of course we should not conclude from this that the citizens in the social body must likewise by subjugated, but let us keep what is valid in the analogy: our cells, like men, need each other.

The organism is a coordinated group allowing the cells—thanks to the unified harmonizing of their functions—to satisfy their needs to the best advantage, therefore to love each other in a community way, with a love that will go so far as to impose sacrifice on less important elements to reduce their activity, if need be, in order to give priority to the more important functions, notably those of the brain.

But the organism is not only a group of cells, it is an individual as well. What makes the individuality is, on the one hand, the unique origin of sister cells and on the other, the *auto-coordination* of the whole, which means that there are not only the functions of the cells but also the functions of the organism. The organism, which materially exists only in its own cells, has nevertheless an existence of its own that is the life of the whole. So that my cells may breathe—the only real need—my organism breathes and, at a higher level, I am able to control my breathing, since I am conscious of it.

The needs of the cells are taken care of either by regulating internal mechanisms that stabilize the composition of the internal environment by renewing the used-up elements and eliminating waste products in a rhythm accorded to its varying needs, or by instinctual activities that, for instance, allow the work of nourishment to proceed. These defense mechanisms of the organic machine are a genuine mechanism of self-love. Our unity has an affective dimension: we feel good when we are in a state of health, we are dissatisfied and discontented when we are in a state of need. Our unity is definitively ensured by the regulating centers of the base of the brain—the real centers of the unity of defense and of unconscious self-love.

This is the pinnacle of the individual bio-love begun at conception and expressed in the organ of bio-love, the central organ of the internal auto-regulations and of the instinctual and affective automatisms—that is, the primitive brain, notably hypothalamus and rhinencephalon. This is, in the human sense, an unconscious bio-love awakening to an obscure bio-consciousness yet expressed at two levels: the physiological level of organic regulation, and the psychophysiological level of instinctive behavior.

What clearly confirms the importance of the unconscious in love is that our affectivity, which for us takes the form of the feeling—the consciousness that we have of it—is at first an unconscious automatism bound up with the functional modalities of our primitive brain. This primitive brain sends its repercussion through the whole organism in order to manifest our emotion and we become conscious of this perturbation when its repercussion reaches our higher brain. There is something of this on the sexual plane, as we have discussed in our books *La Vie sexuelle* and *Apprendre à aimer*. There erotism is at first the unconscious activity of the genital centers of the primitive brain, through the sexual hormones, leading to the automatism of search-for-a-partner, and of courtship followed by the physiological automatism of copulation. In fact the subject is not initially a lover seeking a partner and voluntarily directing the activity of its genital organs, but an automatism set loose in the lower brain compelling entrance into relation with another and pairing off.

With the lower animal this erotic automatism does not comprise the true relations with another that usually go by the name of love. The female of the moth emits an odor that stimulates the male. He is not urged by the conscious sight of the female but unconsciously by the odor. It is nevertheless the unconscious beginning of love. And the transition is graduated as a result of the progress of the higher brain, which allows of passing to mutual knowledge manifested among the birds and the mammals, who are capable of loving one another truly in a conscious interindividual relation. But this higher level progressing toward a true interpsychological love superimposes itself upon the automatisms of the lower brain, which continue to exist and to direct behavior. The animal recognizes another and chooses it, while a specific automatism continues to regulate its behavior.

With man, as we have seen, it is this level of automatic, unconscious love that is diminished, so that it yields no more than the physiological reactions man must learn to satisfy through the higher brain. With man, the bio-love and bio-erotisms are lesser by comparison with their animal counterparts, for in man the psychological dimension has risen to the higher level of love ensured through the higher brain, and it is this level that governs the satisfying of the need. This higher level of animal psychism consists in a positive consciousness, a positive control over the auto-defense mechanisms of the bio-love. This is the germ of conscious love, of the genuine love that, thanks to the higher brain, allows a constitutive love to emerge from the automatic levels and to submit to the responsibility of the individual's own need for love—though always under the control of an unconscious automatic wisdom that compels him to love correctly. It is this unconscious wisdom that disappears in the case of man, since his organism no longer knows how to love in order to satisfy its needs. Man retains the mechanism, but the higher brain is free to use it in any way, even to the detriment of the best interest of the organism. Through ignorance man turns the animal organ of wisdom (which in his case has been liberated for the greater wisdom that *should* result from being submitted to reflection) into an instrument of madness by his refusal to reflect, by his creation of false needs and his immoral way of satisfying such needs.

And so it may be seen that in man's case love should not mean the satisfying of an emotional whim, even though it be of the order of love; love should mean discovering what is most suited to the development of his being. It follows that however altruistic love may be, to love is first of all to love oneself, for a being whose very fabric is love needs love. Consequently the liberty allowed us by our brain is not the absurd power to do just anything we like. Its purpose is to make us discern what is good for us in view of the fact that we are human beings, and to allow us to enter into that good with enthusiasm. To choose with reflection, and to love the good chosen by cells and animals in an unconscious bio-love, is the love function of our brain, the organ by means of which we are no longer simply individuated but become a person.

Comparative psychophysiology is concerned not to describe the habits of all animals, but to enable us the situate the human mutation from the step of reflection within this perspective of *evolutionary progress* that has prepared it. This involves not animals *and* man, but the animal succession that culminates in its extension—man; the confrontation between the progress of individual unity and spirit and the progress of the brain. It involves progress in individualization and the mastery of behavior that is the index of intelligence; and this is not only a progress of steadily emerging consciousness but also a progress of love. It involves the stages of this animal love which at first—on the level of such conditions as relations with another, with the sexual partner or the young—is no more than a simple automatism of tropism and of reflex, but which with the development of the brain (especially among birds and mammals) can evolve into a deliberate individual choice, a genuine love.

But just as this love depends on the human brain to reach the level of totally reflective love freed from innate automatisms, it can also become debased in the automatisms of evil usage or denaturalizing compromise. Man, the only being *capable of loving totally,* is also the only being who can hate totally, who can pervert love into the worst neuroses or the worst frenzies or the worst apathies.

For us who would be human, then, to love is to accept this duty of behaving as a human by committing ourselves to the total development of our person vis-à-vis our state of life. It is to do what one should by reason of what one is, but it is also to do what one should in order to *become* what one is and would not otherwise be. To be humanized or to be dehumanized is to be *amorized* or to be *de-amorized.*

To love, therefore, is to behave as a human and not as an animal or an angel; it is to be faithful to one's place in the animal succession (in the evolutionary sense). It is thus to make complete and correct use of one's brain by giving primacy to the higher brain, and in circumstances in which the human level of love can be attained through reflective and impassioned involvement in the service of the good.

To love means, for one who is normal, to behave normally and not, through ignorance, negligence, or laziness, abnormally—that is, as one incapable of loving freely and humanly because pathologically determined by hormonal disorders or conflicts of the unconscious. We bring on these states by not learning how to love and by refusing to reflect or to be involved in good, in favor of keeping to our unwholesome, conformist habit of fragmented and dissociated love in which the spiritual and physical are divorced.

To love is to be *well reared* in the full sense of the word— that is, to be a genuine *adult* who knows what it means to be a human respecting both himself and his fellows, and who tries to live up to that standard. It is to understand that just as the normal person sometimes conducts himself more abnormally than the abnormal person, so too the real adult is a very rare article, for since we have never understood love and liberty we are still slaves and rebellious adolescents. We obey and we disobey without understanding.

To be an adult does not happen of its own accord; it is not the simple automatism of growing bigger. Learning to be free is bound to be hard work, since it involves learning to use our wills and to control ourselves. And this is achieved neither through an authoritarian training hedged about with prohibitions and taboos, nor through a non-training resulting in the excessive freedom that produces juvenile and post-juvenile delinquents who are incapable of loving since they are not *existing* in the full sense of the word. No one who has not been really loved—whether he has been treated as slave or idol (for these amount to the same thing)—can know how to love, since he does not know how to love himself or how to find out what is right for him and to involve himself in it.

To love is, in fact, to be civilized, which is not at all to have received a scientific and technical education or a course of ethics. Just as the child must learn to develop as a being through efforts that do not cease once he has reached adult status but must continue all his life—which is another way of saying that he must *learn* to love—so too must humanity go on learning in the course of its successive generations. Certainly, since his mutation from the step of reflection, man has had all the human aptitudes, has been capable of loving at the human level. But in the human species a *cultural* evolution extends the biological evolution on another plane. It is a matter, too, of an ascent of love through a fuller realization of the aptitudes of human nature and of the brain's potentialities.

This personalization of love that distinguishes the passage from animal to man was rudimentary in the beginning, since man had barely emerged into individuality in the primitive tribe. Man has to learn to love better than in this primitive form that did not allow his full potentialities to emerge. The tragedy is that instead of progressing, he regresses and develops not his personality but his egoism (his own, or that of institutions of which he has become the worshiping slave) . The natural jungle is replaced by the social jungle; the community disappears and the individual is lost in an indifferent crowd; will power and self-mastery are replaced by a technocracy that treats man as an animal or as a thing. Despite scientific and technological progress, the man who calls himself civilized is sometimes less civilized than the man he despises as a savage yet often knows better than he does how to love. Civilization came about in order to give man a social milieu that would be more beneficial and *amorizing* than the termitary. But more often it places him in conditions wholly perverting and dehumanizing.

The conservative is foolish to lament a past in which man was unable to grow into a complete love, but he is right in his appraisal of current trends. It is not that we should cultivate a love of change, but that we should attain conditions of true progress which are a progress of love. The _noosphere_ proposed by Teilhard as a difficult yet inevitable challenge, is a society of human expansion in which all relations and institutions will be based upon love; it is in a certain sense an _agaposphere_. Unfortunately it is not for the realization of this society that modern technology has become increasingly an insane technocracy dehumanizing both earth and man. And the tragedy is that this dehumanization is not something men want, but arises from our ignorance about what is good for us in view of our nature, and from our ignorance of the depths of love at the heart of our being, a love we must pursue (through good hygiene) or perish.

We have seen how today a complete psychobiological science could make us understand this love if we once made up our minds to ask that of it, and if most of the scientists were not refusing, on the basis of an out-of-date positivism, to structure so all-embracing a discipline.

Matter and Spirit

In the struggle with idealism and angelism and Manicheism we must insist upon this material, physical aspect of love, but not forgetting that physical love is human only when it is also spiritual. In the name of science we must abstract from this _complete love_ the value common to all men, "materialistic" as well as "spiritual." This is not because a complete science could reveal to us the objective values of love through a complete, objective knowledge of the material conditions of subjective reality, which the material study of beings is bound to confuse with a metaphysical materialism. Because modern science does not rely on a description of material phenomenology but is a true _scientific ontology,_ it postulates logically a metaphysical enquiry into the origin of these mysterious powers of matter which go considerably beyond what could be expected from matter in the usual sense. This is because it is less a question of matter than of _organized_ matter, and the more organized it is, the more charged with spiritual powers it becomes.

Sixty years ago one could oppose to a simplistic materialism, which denied the spiritual, a spiritualism that confirmed the evident existence of this spiritual aspect but could still add it on to simple matter. But today one can no longer oppose just any kind of spiritualism to the realist materialism that recognizes the spiritual as a property of matter and makes it an argument against the separate existence of the spirit and its immortality. The spiritualism that added spirit on to insufficient matter seemed to make it a useless superstructure.

So today it is not about the insufficiency of matter that one must reason, but about the _relations of its sufficiency and of its organization._ Metaphysics should expound to us the scientific law that out of quantitative complexification new qualities apparently arise. Now, such a metaphysic of organization was not invented for the needs of the occasion, for it is precisely that *hylomorphism* which St. Thomas borrowed (completing and rectifying it) from Aristotle. (We have discussed this in *Notre corps, ce mystère* [Paris, 1962].) As we know, this involves a metaphysic in which the organization of matter is explained by its *informing* principle. It agrees perfectly with modern science in that the unity of the being is respected and is not split into matter and spirit; thus man is not a body and a soul, but an *ensouled* body, the presence of the soul as a constituent of the body being seen in the organization-complexity of the body and of the brain.

For anyone observing the psychological difference between non-reflective animal psychism and reflective human psychism, the step of reflection involves the threshold separating the true spirit from its preparation. But this spiritual being is an *incarnate* spiritual being that manifests itself in the organization and powers of a material structure, but is in no way condemned to disappear with it at death. The agreement of science and of Thomism may be observed in the gradations of organization and of *information* from the inanimate to man in which the Thomist principles of the substantial form, of the vegetable and animal soul, and of the human soul perfectly account for the differences between the properties of inanimated matter and living matter, animal psychism and human psychism. It is the difference in the nature of the *informing* principle that we must link to the power of complexification to condition new qualities. Thus the most precious principle of Marxist dialectical materialism takes its ultimate logical interpretation from Thomist philosophy.

Thomism, not in possession of the modern scientific concept of evolution, was of course limited to a static picture of the different degrees of being which, as we know today, must be seen rather in a historical dynamism. The substantial form prepared for the appearance of the non-spiritual soul, and this in turn prepared for the coming of the spirit. But the Thomist philosophy of substantial form should be completed today in a context that would give it its full dimension, which is of the order of love.

As Teilhard saw very clearly, the metaphysic of organization—that is, the unity superimposed on the variable elements—must allow more for the dynamism of unitive attractions than for the simple form: we need a *metaphysic of union.* Just as, scientifically, we learn that organic integration is not only bio-consciousness but also bio-love, so, metaphysically, it is easy to *amorize* the concept of form. The properties of matter make love-energy the secret of the universe, and, indeed modern physics is in the process of measuring it under the form of energy-measure, precisely from the data in which we may confirm the Teilhardian concept of radial energy: the energy of centration and unification.

Such a metaphysic of organization via *amorization* logically brings up the mystery of its source. For this progress of love manifested in the progress of organization and causing an immanent love to advance to the stage of the emergence of truly spiritual and reflective love, should lead the unbeliever to suspect the existence of a transcendence at the source of this *amorization.* As Teilhard says, if matter in evolution demonstrates such an ascent of love right up to the emergence of personal human love, shouldn't that lead us, not to *prove,* but to *envisage as logical* the hypothesis that the secret Mover of the evolution is a God who is personal and who is love? Not a God-love added on to a world without love, but a God-love whose transcendence is expressed in the secret presence immanent in His work, which is the true God. Not a magician acting from outside with the purpose of moulding the world, but the

First Cause delegating His powers to secondary causes—the properties of matter that He respects.

The believer who knows that this is God's way of creating, by His secret presence and the delegation of His powers, should not be surprised to find love inhering in such a creation. He need not be reminded that God is love since Revelation has already told him that, but in this presence of love in the world now scientifically recognized he finds confirmation of his faith. And thus he is forewarned of the idealist, angelist, Manichean temptation to separate matter from spirit, the world from God.

In this union of the science of love and the theology of love we thus achieve the integration of faith-in-the-world (which we must complete by *amorization* inasmuch as we are co-creators) and faith-in-God (who delegates His powers to us).

CHAPTER 3

THE DUTY TO EXIST

THERE IS NO LOFTIER MORAL precept than to love one's neighbor as oneself. But we do not understand its full significance. We have the idea that loving our neighbor has been imposed as a duty because it is not our natural tendency, and that the whole intent of the command is satisfied by the ends of either living in peace or obeying God. But then why the criterion *as oneself?* This would seem to imply that the other person should be as dear to me as what I hold closest to my heart—namely, my own self, without which I should not exist at all. Isn't this unnatural, to will to put the other person—the stranger, this neighbor who is so remote—into the very place I myself occupy? And if I love him as myself, can I still love myself completely?

There seems to be some incompatibility between these two commandments, and in actual fact, some people love only themselves or at least love themselves more than their neighbor, while others practice self-forgetfulness so thoroughly as to devote themselves to and live entirely for others. Isn't this the attitude that moral philosophy should encourage? For if it is necessary to love one's neighbor as oneself, it is equally necessary to love oneself—and isn't this an invitation to egoism? It is easy to go to extremes; it is easy to obliterate everything in one's frenzied quest of selfish pleasures—and not even see the victims one destroys. It is easy, too, to burn with zeal for self-abnegation and charity. The rule of the wise middle way of synthesis by which one loves others without forgetting self is one that hardly tempts us. Yet this happy medium should strike us as the only reasonable approach, for it is the only one that is at once difficult and rewarding. It is much more worthwhile (albeit arduous) to struggle along the high ridge than to topple down the precipice to one side or the other.

It is wrong to love oneself by forgetting others, but it is equally wrong to forget oneself completely in order to love others more. Moral theology has plainly shown us the sinfulness of egoism (though it still remains acutely tempting); but we have not understood that there is also a temptation to sin in excessive altruism. We must not love others too much, for that is to love them badly, and with a love that is contrary to our nature. Conversely, egoism is loving oneself too much, and therefore badly. There is, however, a duty to *love oneself adequately*. Thus, a healthy morality postulates primarily the self-evident truth that *we have a duty to love ourselves.*

And this makes sense, for in fact egoism consists in being

unable to love oneself, just as much as does excessive altruism. But how can this be? We know the answer, now that neurophysiological investigations have demonstrated for us the human significance of love. Loving another person, like loving ourselves, is not achieved by performing actions as a duty to a love external to ourselves—*manufacturing* love, so to speak. What is necessary is *to be love.*

As we have seen, love is the supreme property that makes persons of us. One who wants to love without *being love* is not capable of loving. But one who is in a state of love—or rather (for nothing is static and passive), one who is in a state of progress toward greater love, that is, in a state of *amorization*—could not possibly act in contradiction to what he is. His duty is not to love but to *be love:* to love is only the consequence or the medium of *being love.* And this is to love oneself. It can be seen, then, that *it is no longer possible to dissociate love of another from love of oneself:* the personal love of the person *who is love* compels him to love everything. To love the other person requires an "I" love that could hardly fail to love itself; the self-love of the person *who is love* embraces within it the love of others.

To be love is to be an authentic person working toward the growth of his nature, that vocation of love with which he is marked. It is only natural to be loving because one *is* love. But for all that, the fact that it is natural does not necessarily mean that it is easy. It is not easy to follow a vocation. To be humanly "natural" requires a difficult effort of intelligence and perseverance. Love is a duty, but a duty of faithful self-realization, a duty of hygiene and health.

To love is to be. And that seems easy. We already exist, we say. But that is where we make our mistake: we do not exist in the full sense of the word. We undergo existence without being fully conscious of it. We live without *reflective consciousness of existing.* Man has the duty to exist fully; otherwise he is not a man. It is the animal who does not have the power to exist fully and does not need it, for the automatisms of his body cause him to be and to do what is suited to him, in an unconscious bio-love. Whereas in man, as we have seen, reflective existence must replace the deficient automatisms. At the summit of his being, man should replace the automatic bio-love of animal existence with the reflective love of human existence. The animal is guided by his hypothalamic infraconscious individuality; man uses the brain of love, the prefrontal, to *love consciously*, which is to ensure his fully human status.

This authentic existence is not too common, for it does not depend automatically upon our constitution; we must also have learned to use our brain. And one does not learn this by forcing oneself to love others, nor by abandoning oneself to egotistical impulses. To learn how to love does not primarily require that one repress one's own egoism and concern oneself with others.

The duty of love is a duty to *be love*, a duty to *exist fully*. Hence in this purview we are not existing. Modern man would say: I act, therefore I am. But he would do better to say: I think, therefore I am; for it is necessary to think before acting. But we are putting the emphasis on the verb. For existence the essential is not to think and to act; the essential is the I who directs the thought and the action. It is essential to learn *to be an I* who is existing and commanding. For our natural tendency is to be a quasi non-existent "I" who simply submits to existence while deluded that we are "calling the shots."

The egoist believes in loving himself, and the moralist is tempted to reproach him with his sin. God alone is the judge of the degree of our responsibility, but it is certainly lessened (if not excused) by our ignorance. The egoist is the prey of excessive impulsiveness that prevents him from loving himself truly, from existing fully. Unaware as he is of his true need of self-love, unaware of the others he alienates, he runs the risk of making up for his loss by sadistic excesses. On the other hand, the person who thinks he is loving others properly by neglecting himself may be obeying a variety of mixed motives from which egoism is not entirely absent. The unconscious rejection of authentic love can lead to the way of masochism on the part of such a person, for he loves in order to mortify himself by positing a false love.

Before acting it is essential to learn *to be,* for only one who has learned to be can fully control his actions, only he can be free. If freedom is uncommon it is not because we have no aptitude for it, but because we have not learned to make use of it. What we think we want is the impulses and intuitions that come to us from our hormones, from our drives, from our complexes, from our habits, from our prejudices. Whereas freedom consists in reflecting before acting, and therefore in self-mastery as opposed to the spontaneity with which it is so often confused. Freedom is fidelity to our true nature in the struggle against the unconstraint that seems natural to us. It is the play of intelligence on my behavior, an intelligence that leads me to choose what is suitable to me: not according to my whims (which would be alienation in the automatisms) but what is suited to me because it is good for me. And what is good for me is what is first of all humanly good in a general way since, insofar as I am an individual, I am first and foremost human.

Animal psychology grades the degree of intelligence in an animal not by the perfection of the actions, which can only be automatisms either instinctive or acquired, but by the capacity for self-control to the end of acting in a better way by making use of its experience. The intelligence is the mastery of behavior that allows us to choose the highest good; it is the mark of the superior animal capable of *détour,* i.e., of keeping hands off the object of his desire or of being forcibly kept from it, of executing a preparatory action without immediate relation to the end in view, in order to be more certain of attaining that end.

Animal intelligence counterbalances the deficiencies of the instincts by allowing the animal to improve his behavior and to adapt himself better to new conditions. Human intelligence, which is greatly superior, is the more indispensable in that it entirely supplants the instinct. Human intelligence is a matter of finding the good, forming the habit of seeking it, and therefore knowing what to love so as to be fully human—i.e., a being not bound by what he loves in a bio-love, but choosing what he should love through this reflective love that is the glory of the human person.

To know how to love to the end of existing fully is an aptitude of human provenance, and yet it has never been and never will be easy to achieve. Primitive man in other times sloughed off the responsibility to do so on to social customs, but this conformism could be a very dehumanizing mistake. It is reasonable for modern man to want to be free and no longer to obey. But since he ignores the conditions and implications of his freedom, he ends up being less free than our primitive man, and more the slave of his most elementary impulses, which good social mores, despite their inadequacy and irreflectiveness, used to hold in check. Rejecting legalism, man thrusts aside at the same time the legality of his being. So, confident that in so far as he is civilized he exists more fully, is more a free subject and more *responsible* than primitive man bound by the taboos of his tribe, modern man is not really existing at all, for what he calls free will is actually only his physical drives and his prejudices—conformist or anti-conformist as they may be.

His capacity to exist is further reduced to the extent that the unhygienic conditions of his life make him vulnerable to *nervous fatigue*, for this exhaustion disturbs the auto-regulative centers of his brain, causing him to lose all control of himself. (On this point, see my work, *La Fatigue* [Paris, 1956].) On the other hand, for fear of falling into the disequilibrium of an authoritarian education—a training contrary to liberty—he commits

himself to an excessive libertarianism which, with its morbid
dread of complexes and its rejection of standards, fails to teach
the child to control himself and thus to make use of his potentialities for freedom.

Granted the brain man has been given, he has to learn all the
vital actions; but no one teaches them to him. This apprenticeship in knowing how to feel, how to will, how to rest, how to
sleep, how to observe, is summed up in *knowing how to exist:*
learning truly to be, knowing how to love oneself. Now we have
not really understood what we know in this area. We have
stopped at the stage of the infant who learned to be by making
use of his brain while playing in his cradle.

During the first two or three years of life, while the cerebral
nervous system is developing, the child learns to make use of his
potentialities. He learns the meaning of the messages from the
senses by learning to distinguish his ego from the external
world; and he learns to coordinate his movements in order to
perform certain gestures. Having formed in his brain the image
of his body—the cerebral ego—he learns to make it the subject
of sensations that have become conscious and of actions that
have become voluntary; he learns to utilize his cerebral potentialities for observation, concentration, imagination. In this
way he sets up for himself the *basic equipment* for human
behavior. But the potentialities of this infantile consciousness,
which he develops by exercising his functions, remain minimal.

Since after infancy people do not continue developing in this
direction (since indeed they consider their training to be
finished), to be conscious and to will are regarded as *properties*
of the brain and thus not calling for any special exercises to
develop them. Consequently all we possess for coping with
adult problems is the cerebral control of the child. In the course
of his play the child put forth immense effort to develop his
perceptions and to coordinate his movements, to observe and to
will. We adults acquired the habit, and we think that we are

doing these things to perfection—which is far from the case. To be adult we must resume at adult level the exercises of the child.

To will seems to us to require the exercise of a considerable—and often ineffectual—spiritual energy in order to dominate and mortify a rebellious flesh. This is because we do not know how to will. To will is to know how to control our brain in order to dominate its functioning by making the cerebral self, as it were, the subject of our sensations, our actions, our thoughts, our imaginings. That necessitates learning how to observe more keenly, how to control ourselves, how to eliminate useless thoughts. We are the prey, the more so when we are fatigued, of cerebral vagrancy. We have in our brain wonderful dispositions for feeling, for willing, for conscious awareness; and we let them function in any old way without making use of their full potentialities. That is why we do not *exist*. These powers exist in us and yet we barely advert to them and hardly ever master them. Faced with the difficulty of exerting will power and self-mastery, we avoid the effort without once grasping that it would be easy if we had learned how, and that it would still be easy to learn.[1]

But we do not realize that one who cannot exert his will and master himself is a non-existent, because the true name for mastery is the fulfillment and expansion of the person. The moralist reproaches us for our sins without allowing for the fact that the full responsibility for fully willing evil is not within our power. Quite simply, we are incapable of resisting temptation because we have not learned how to do so. We are not even capable of the reflective intelligence that would make obvious to us the stupid incoherence of our behavior and the evident

---

1. For more on this point, see my discussions in *La maîtrise de soi* (Paris, 1963) and its bibliography, and in *Conduite de soi et Progrès humain* (Paris, 1965).

perniciousness of the evil that lies not in harmful exterior behavior but in the perversion of our being.

To know how to will in order to *exist* is the secret of the
Oriental techniques of Yoga and Zen, which show us that the
will is not a constricting exertion, but a positive relaxing that
does not "will" in the usual sense. It is a paradox that we
should find this secret of existence in the mystics, who otherwise
dream of dissolving in an impersonal "great all," but this is
because the secret of existence is primarily the struggle against
egoism. Herrigel relates the counsels of a Zen archery master to
the tensed Western man who hopes to send his arrow to the
target but fails, of course. The arrow has to go by itself, the
subject applying himself not to his action but to being perfectly
calm and relaxed.

What reveals very clearly the extent of our inability to will is
that it would seem astonishing to us—and even more so to the
interested party—to tell a woman who was undergoing a normal confinement, or a sufferer who was tossing around in bed
the prey to insomnia, that they had only to will it and the pain
would go, or sleep would come. They may try; but we know
very well that it is impossible. This is simply because we do not
know either how to will or what it means to will.

In reality it is through the will that the pain of the confinement goes or sleep comes. But one must learn beforehand just
what one has to do for that, and what apparently seems irrele-
vant. One does not learn to have a confinement by having a
confinement; what is permitted by the psychoprophylactic
method is, on the one hand, to put aside the prejudice that a
confinement is of necessity and naturally painful, and then to
utilize the body's messages not for suffering pain but for carrying out certain useful activities, as for example, controlling
one's breathing. The woman who has grasped what she should
do does not suffer; she has a voluntary confinement directed by
an educated brain. It is the same with regard to voluntary
sleep. It is not enough to lie down in the dark; one must first

have learned to calm oneself, to condition oneself, to induce sleep by exercises simple but more effective than counting sheep.

What is involved in achieving a confinement without pain, or a sound natural sleep, is the utilization of one's full cerebral resources for willing one's good, for existing more authentically by forbidding oneself to be unhinged by pain or nervous irritation. It is knowing how to love ourselves truly by procuring through our own resources what our body needs, by humanizing our behavior. It is exactly the opposite of what modern man, who does not know how to will, expects of science. He wants medicines and pills. The woman who has been drugged no longer performs with any joy that magnificent function of bringing a child into the world. She is content to suppress both the pain and the consciousness by anaesthesia, which is always dangerous; and the child is born in veterinary fashion with the help of the doctor but without the participation of the mother. In the same way the insomniac stupefies himself with drugs, and is obliged later to wake himself with stimulants that are even more harmful.

To an ever greater extent the "technocrats" will offer us palliatives for our incapacity to master ourselves, instead of techniques for training in self-control. They are on the right side, of course, in their impulse to alleviate our state of nerves; but the lesser evil offered prevents this greater good of utilizing natural resources so as to be truly human. And what is worse, the remedies offered to us purpose to offset the toxic effects of an unhealthful way of life rather than to eliminate the cause. Thus to the harmfulness of the life the harmfulness of the remedies is superadded: insult to injury. It would be better to adopt hygienic habits than to have to justify our harmful nostrums as we do.

We do not know how to will because we have not learned, and we are even less capable of learning now because jangled nerves increase cerebral vagrancy. Paradoxically, we must understand that we can both learn to will and learn to calm ourselves. The twofold effect will be obtained by learning how to "simmer down."

The modern activist in his frenzy of living no longer knows how to live. And he no longer knows how to live because he does not take the time to pause in order to reflect. He can no longer do this. He needs rest, but he states that he has no time for it. Or else he "rests" by taking on some other activity, by wearing himself out on some freeway by speeding and breathing in exhaust fumes, or blowing his horn because he finds himself in a traffic jam, thus increasing his nervous fatigue. So we have no time? Then let us not waste any of it, and let us learn how to "super-rest" in a few minutes.

Since fatigue knots us up, let us be aware of this and learn to relax. Deliberate relaxation of our muscles is achieved by the cerebral control of our regulating centers, and this relaxation calms our upset nerves, for these are the same centers that control the muscles and the brain. By learning to relax, not only do we produce calm in ourselves, but we do so voluntarily by learning to control ourselves. And it is precisely in this that the will consists. The very achievement of relaxing ourselves teaches us to will and engenders in us the clarity of vision and interior peace to recognize the activist stupidity that prevents us from *existing*. This unclouded look at our life will show us our true good and inspire us to seek it. No one, as a matter of fact, desires what is bad for himself and for others, no one seeks to die or to cause death by heart failure. Despite ourselves we are carried along by this world which we have made and of which we are the slaves, a world that must be changed, a world that can be changed if we would only take the time to look at it and to learn the rules of healthful living.

There is too great a tendency to assume that methods of loosening up and relaxation are a form of snobbery indulged in by the "idle rich." More often it is the productive people who need them, for if they hope to change the world they must be able to see clearly what is going wrong, and have enough self-mastery to dedicate themselves to the task of changing it without wasting their energies in the process.

To learn to will by relaxing requires only that one believe sufficiently in the necessity for or the possibility of willing—that is, sufficiently to perform the indicated exercises. These exercises are so simple by comparison with the end in view that we think them simplistic. And we refuse to make use of them, since nothing so simple involves either a real challenge or the pleasure of poisoning oneself with medications.

As a corrective for the aggressiveness of motorists, instead of methods of control which allow a man to see himself and other people clearly, Dr. Henri Laborit recently suggested the elimination by drugs of the instinctual brain, which primitive man needed for self-defense in a hostile world and which we should no longer need. This is a very serious error, for a drug is always toxic, and we need the primitive brain for loving. It must be controlled, not eliminated by drugging.

Several methods of control that teach us how to will and to exist have been proposed in numerous syntheses.[2] Through one or another method, the authors all hope to enable us to take command of our automatisms: methods derived from Yoga, methods of relaxation and of bodily expression. The best, because it is the most complete and the least dangerous, is Dr. Vittoz's method of cerebral control, which is intended to teach us everything that we have not mastered, everything that is in our brain.[3]

It is a matter of escaping from our intellectualist verbalism

2. E.g., P. Chanson, *Pour la santé du corps et de l'esprit* (Paris, 1955), or Marianne Kohler, *Techniques de la sérénité* (Paris, 1963).
3. Only one of Dr. Vittoz's works seems to be available in translation: *Treatment of Neurasthenia*, trans. by H. B. Brooke (London–New York, 1911 and 1921; 7th French ed., 1954). Author cites Dr. Vittoz's own *Le Docteur Roger Vittoz et l'angoisse modern* (Paris, 1965), and Pierre D'Espiney, *La psychothérapie du Dr Vittoz* (Paris, 1965).—*Ed.*

so that we may be penetrated by the "happenings" of nature that get to us through the senses though we are unconscious of them. Let us advert, then to the green of these leaves, to that fragrance, to this song—by educating our receptivity.[4] Let us stop thinking for a moment so that we can take thought for our thought—but it must be thought fixed upon something real and not just a rehashing of our problems. It is a matter of taking joyful cognizance of the wonders of our bodies: this hand, these fingers, feeling their abnormal tension and then slackening it, feeling our movements and then controlling them by making simple and conscious gestures, respirations, controlled movements. And so we shall learn to will and automatically to will in the right way—which is to will the good. For we are so made that the right functioning of our brain adds up to the good, while evil is always composed of natural temptations to denaturalization, of yielding to alienating impulses.

Vittoz teaches us by the simple exercise of evoking mental images how to pay attention, how to control ourselves, how to eliminate without effort whatever distracts us. He goes on to teach us what is supposed to be unteachable and yet is most essential. He teaches us to *exist,* to feel consciously the joy of existing; he teaches us how to assert ourselves, how to view the other person, even how to learn to tolerate him.

The Vittoz method is useful as a method of "synthesis and reconstruction" for the treatment of psychoneuroses (he has published a study in this area [5]) ; but it is quite as useful for re-educating normal people who because of nervous exhaustion or lack of training are becoming more and more psychoneu-

---

4. This sharpening of the senses has been explored by C. D. Boulogne, O.P., *in Mes amis les senses* (Paris, 1951) , translated as *My Friends the Senses* by Jane Hawes (New York, 1953) .—*Ed.*

5. See *Psychothérapie de synthèse et de reconstruction,* by Dr. Vittoz (Paris, 1965) .

THE DUTY TO EXIST

rotic though not suffering from any psychoneuroses. Practicing
these exercises is the best school of will training and humanization, but even more important than practicing them is realizing
the psychophysiological necessity for will training and humanization. For this reason we recommend some "notes and
thoughts" of Dr. Vittoz, for they constitute at once a most
attractive work on spirituality and a manual of psychophysiological health. This is what Dr. Vittoz writes:

"It is by the rightness of the feeling that one recognizes that
an idea is right. It is essential to be able to find relaxation in
correct receptivity of exterior things. That never fails and is
always right: an idea may warp, may escape, may weary. Conscious actions should turn out to be natural to you, to be part of
yourself. Perform conscious actions from month to month and
this way attain to freedom of the will—that is, learn to be
independent of every situation.

"Alongside belief in the truth, there is an even more important, more primordial phenomenon, one that most frequently
escapes the analysis of thinkers, and that is *unity*. We must
enter wholly into what we are doing; this is the way to perfect
our slightest actions. For that we must acquire the unity that
concentrates our energies instead of squandering them at total
loss. Every energy not employed turns against itself. No effort is
lost. The more you work toward unity, the more you will
simplify and the more you will see things on a big scale. Then
everything is in perspective.

"Our purpose is to realize on the moral plane what is done
on the physical plane, to show that consciousness passing from
the physical plane leads inevitably to the moral plane, that
physical equilibrium is the first step toward moral equilibrium.
Every act of control is an advance toward the better. The rules
of control are the rules of perfection. If such control thrusts
toward perfection—and it does not *exact* it (after all, we have
liberty)—it is a demonstration of perfectibility. It is a matter

of showing the subject how, from an act that is purely material at the beginning, he arrives, by the very fact of control, at the most elevated concept from a spiritual viewpoint. All perfecting within our control is a perfecting of moral and physical equilibrium; therefore control in itself is one of the bases of perfectibility. Do we see control in depraved persons? Certainly not. On the other hand, we do see that a certain degree of control accompanies every man who has good moral qualities.

"Every man who hopes to re-educate or strengthen his control must do battle on his weaknesses. One might say that man instinctively retards the growth of his control in order not to have to war against his weaknesses and vices; and then he wonders why he does not feel the happiness that perfect balance bestows. Clearly, insofar as he has not overcome his worst tendencies he cannot be completely stable. Whatever is troubling him is somehow wrong and derives from a lack of control. Therefore when one thing troubles you, eliminate that; for, however good it may be in itself, it remains wrong in relation to you until you are able to objectify it without doubt or disturbance. One must always know how to dominate what is below the self." (From "Notes et pensées," in *Le Docteur Roger Vittoz et l'angoisse moderne.*)

Indeed Vittoz seems like a moralist of the brain; and while the exercises he proposes are essential—for to believe one must make the attempt—more important still is the spirit he gives us, the spirit in which we must practice the different methods. He shows us what we must do if we want to *exist* and set out with enthusiasm on the most wonderful of adventures, one that will go on until the end of humanity—the conquest of self, the realization of the self-ideal.

Some people might see in all this a manifestation of egoism, if they have not understood that it is a matter of an ascesis of struggle against egoism, but a human and a balanced ascesis that does not confuse the renunciation and mortification of egoism with renunciation of being or of existing or being happy. It is all a matter of seeing ourselves clearly. And this is to see our greatness, and our free dignity, yes, but at the same time our limitations, our fragility, our weakness. It is a matter of accepting ourselves for what we are, in order to love ourselves truly in willing our own good. And what we are is *neither nothing nor everything;* it is the human condition that is not animal, nor thing, nor God.

We must avoid the temptation to two really serious alienations—the one of overestimating ourselves and the other of underestimating ourselves. Both lead to our lying to ourselves and to bringing about serious disturbances: the disturbance of the man who styles himself, and longs to be, superior while he knows in his heart that he is not, and that of the man who through humility wants to be too inferior and who throws himself out of balance at the opposite end of this false and untenable position. The moral theologian rejects the excesses of the one who puts himself in God's place—a false and tyrannical god—and who is proud and vain and egoistic. But unilateral denunciation of this excess makes us see good in the opposite, which is only another excess—this time, of humility and humiliation—that amounts to rejection of the joy of existence.

To be above the maximum or to be below the minimum is equally unbalancing. Balance demands the middle position, which rejects both too much pride and too much humility; which does not confuse healthy *amour-propre* and dignity with harmful pride, and does not equate the struggle against egoism with a rejection of the ego. If the danger of pride is greater than that of the inverse sin of excessive humility, it is because we have naturally such a perverse tendency to manifest our ego in exaggerated fashion and we draw such satisfaction from it without reckoning the danger. Whereas, if our humility has not gone so far as to pitch us into hopeless, abject misery, it can be checked by a legitimate rebellion on our part. But that rebellion for its part goes too far when it leads the humbled person to pride and arrogance in asserting his rights. On the other hand, to go after an excessive humility for the sake of mortification and penance is just as dangerous.

This middle way of clear recognition of what one is, by avoiding vicious or pseudo-virtuous excesses, is the secret of self-love as opposed to either egoism or complete self-abnegation. It is to be found not only in this virtue of existing rightly, but also in all our ways of behaving. To exist rightly comprises acting rightly, and this obviously eliminates the fault of laziness, but equally the fault of activism. To act rightly is to avoid acting without reflection—if need be, to appear lazy while considering what should be done. For laziness, of course, is another way of acting without reflection, or in refusing to move from thought to action. Where action is called for, then, man is tempted to take either too much action or too little; whereas what he must do is to seek the middle way of clear action, which is good action and action directed toward the good.

And this action looks to obtaining some result. Here again we find the same dilemma: man has a tendency to want too much and, if he adverts to it, he will endeavor to possess too little. Excess of riches and excess of poverty and privation are contrary to love of self. Anyone who hasn't enough has a right to protest, without bearing too great a grudge; but one who has too much should become conscious of the wrongness of his situation, too.

To love oneself means to seek the optimum—the golden mean—with enthusiasm, difficult though this is; for this optimum permits self-conquest and self-realization, one's own expansion. But here again, we prefer the non-optimum, squandering our enthusiasm upon a quest for immoderate power, or, on the other hand, upon some position we believe to constitute moral perfection but is really fanaticism about mortification to the point of abjection. This is usually characterized by a rejection of all passion, of all enthusiasm, of all emotion: an inhuman and unbalanced detachment of no more value than an excessive attachment. A passion for passion, one might call it, as Etienne Borne has said of the passion for truth that is passionately pursued—and crucified—in the splitting asunder of contending schools of thought. (See his *Passion de la verité* [Paris, 1962].—*Ed.*)

If we want to understand how the optimum becomes the condition for authentic existence, we must turn to biology, for here we are shown, on an elementary level, that this cerebral balance demands an optimum of all the physical or chemical factors, too much being as harmful as too little. The law of the optimum, which is the basis of morality, was recognized by the physiologist Paul Bert, father of cosmic medicine (1833–86), when he established that an excess of oxygen, the vital gas, was as harmful as an insufficiency of it. To reach a high altitude without the protection of an oxygen mask or an airtight cabin leads to psychic trouble, to coma and death through lack of oxygen; but to swim in the deep exposes one to the toxicity of oxygen under pressure that triggers convulsions with loss of consciousness. This optimum is to be found everywhere, with vitamins, hormones, internal temperature (the ravings of fever and the coma of extreme cold) ; with noise (a leading factor in nervous disorders) and the total absence of noise, which, when achieved in soundproof chambers, is psychologically even more upsetting. This law of our cerebral functioning is encountered in all our psychic and social activity conditioned by the brain, and explains the dangers of too much as well as too little in being, just as in acting and in having.

The tragedy of the world as we know it, where we cannot will our good because of our ignorance of hygiene, is that the underprivileged, who are justly dissatisfied, aim to attain the level of excessive wealth, since they too are as unconscious as the wealthy of the fact that excess of riches is not suited to our make-up. To make the whole world rich would be impossible; as a matter of actual fact, it is not desirable. To take pity on the disadvantaged and to help them emerge from their poverty is an obvious duty. Yet the idea of rescuing the rich would never occur to anyone, though they are unconsciously doing themselves harm with their riches and we should extricate them from their imbalanced state by helping them to understand it.

We know how Christianity has rightly insisted upon the spirit of poverty and the dangers of excess wealth. Unfortunately, people have read into this a mandated ascesis of mortification, when what should primarily concern us is to bring about conditions healthful for human balance and to conform with what is good for us and leads us to a more authentic existence. What we need is moderation in all things, even in moderation.

To seek the optimum in *being*, in *acting*, and in *having* can be envisaged only as we have just envisaged it from the viewpoint of the individual caught between the inclinations toward too much and toward too little. But for human beings living in society, our approach to self-love necessarily has repercussions upon our relations with others. To take one's own place, therefore, means taking it in relation to others in whatever way favors the optimum in the social ambience. But to state that man is a social species is not only to state that men are in relations of coexistence and collaboration; it is also to recognize in ourselves a need of others which must also be oriented toward the optimum. This is what we are going to study now, demonstrating how self-love in a social species necessarily involves love of others, and in what this love consists.

CHAPTER 4

WE NEED ONE ANOTHER

OUR IGNORANCE of the fact that we are not alone on earth but are members of human societies that together make up humanity is on a par with our unenlightened self-assessment as we have discussed it above. We have to grasp that legitimate self-assertion or self-defense does not mean a craving for unlimited self-aggrandizement of the sort that morality urges us to check by means of chastening self-forgetfulness. But it does demand that we wisely keep it within limit at the cost of a difficult ascesis. But again, this is a mortification of egoism only, and

exercise   69

otherwise expresses rather the positive aspect of *being* authentically and of knowing how to love ourselves in the truth of *being,* of *acting,* of *having.*

Our life instinct, urging us on to unlimited expansion, makes other people appear to us as enemies, as competitors. Because their desires coincide and clash with ours, and thus limit them, they prevent us from too much *being, having,* or *acting.* But it is not in conflict and hatred that a sound social order will be realized, nor will it be brought about by indifference that strains to preserve its isolation at all costs. We *need* one another. The Judeo-Christian law of loving one's neighbor as oneself must be explained and thoroughly understood. For this law is not a matter of God's imposing some incomprehensible duty on us for the sake of our salvation—a sort of beneficent penance. A whole scientific discipline would be required for a really objective explanation of not only our need of others but also our need (and hence our duty) to love them as well.

There is ambiguity in this word "need." The herbivorous animal needs grass, and the wolf needs the lamb; but this is in order to devour it, to assimilate its substance, to change its nature, to subject it to the law of its own nucleic acids and to make it part of itself. In fact for us, too, the other person can be an object to *use,* a prey on whom we exercise our will to power, even though this be under the guise of love. People speak of wanting to "devour" someone very dear, and this implies an appetite for possession utterly opposed to the respect for liberty that should prevail in an interpersonal relation. To have "one's own" poor is to desire the welfare of certain people in our own fashion and one quite unconnected with their personal initiative—a form of altruism that is seriously contaminated with egoism.[1] Nothing is more characteristic of all this than the

---

1. This basically romantic attitude is named "charitism" by Maynooth sociologist Jeremiah Newman in *Change and the Catholic Church* (Baltimore, 1965). It was also examined by Catholic University's William J. Kerby in *The Social Mission of Charity* (New York, 1921).—*Ed.*

peculiar changes in the meaning of the word "subject," which was used originally to denote the human person in command of his actions but now designates the slave of the master's wishes, the person in a state of subjection and stripped of all liberty.

To assert power excessively is to exceed the golden mean and to become imbalanced. In the relation between the tyrant and the slave—and it would be the same if the tyrant were a god and the slave his willing servitor—there is not one unbalanced person but two, too little (as we have said) being as harmful as too much. Because we need the other person this does not mean that he is to be reduced to the state of slavery for our benefit—or for his benefit, as we might envisage it. The other person is not our pretext to be egotistical, for our salvation or for his—which is a peculiar and very common way of being falsely altruistic.

Yet perhaps it is better to have a false need for others than to be altogether unconscious of human interdependence. Now, on the one hand, man has a very positive tendency to dominate the other person, and he reacts against this by means of altruism that is often only a new form of domination in the name of what is good. This of course is not to say that no good accrues, only that each person must be helped to consent freely to it. On the other hand he has a no less perverse tendency—his need for *solitude*, his desire to be, to do, and to have, solely for himself.

Man is a de-socialized being—which is to say that interdependence appears to him as moral constraint to which he may choose, or not, to subject himself. While the other person often appears as a competitor to be envied, the will to ignore him is a much more serious matter. We are quite ready to accept being indebted to society, but what we do not seem to realize is that society has no existence of its own as such, that it is composed of other men. What characterizes our era is the isolation of the individual in the crowd. He suffers from a lack of love and of really *human* relations, but he is not conscious of it.

Our most serious presumption is to think that we can acquire true balance while living in isolation and neglecting, envying, despising, or destroying others.

Today we set ourselves against both the social and the individual, and we see in socialization the threat of oppression while quite ignoring the serious dehumanization that befalls one who discounts the social dimension. To love the other person is not a moral rule or regulation in the usual sense of the word; it is an absolute necessity of our nature. We are made for this end and we seriously unbalance ourselves when we contravene it by hatred or indifference.

Before we can understand all this, we must understand exactly what is meant by a social species. On the ground that human sociology concerns a distinct species distinguishing this discipline from animal sociology, there is a tendency to separate the two species as well. It is quite accurate to state that only human society maintains social institutions having an existence of their own and capable of being studied in themselves. Precisely, human society is cultural and does not rest, like animal societies, upon unchanging social customs and coercive social instincts. In humankind there are varying social customs in the different societies that succeed each other in time or coexist on earth.

But why oppose the cultural to the biological? why conclude that the human cultural dimension, the social plasticity of his customs, implies that man is not a natural creature? It is the nature of man in virtue of the constitution of his brain to develop by means of culture. A man without culture would be an abnormal man, a denaturalized man; for from his very beginning, man, the social species, has had a culture however primitive. What distinguishes man is that his is the only biological heredity by chromosomes of which we do not know whether what has been acquired may be determined by the cultural heredity of educational transmission, of transmission of techniques by apprenticeship, or transmission of traditions and customs by word. But this cultural heredity is by no means purely sociological and cut off from the biological; it is rather the social method of utilizing the potentialities of man's brain. Our thought is interior language—that is, we think with the words of the language we have received from our environment, from other people. We can see, then, to what extent the biological side of our make-up needs the social side if we are to call ourselves human.

But the social human is not a commonplace biological fact; he is inserted into a *human bio-sociology.* Thus, whether one considers only the biological aspect while ignoring the social, or else sees only the social while ignoring the bio-sociological, one risks failing to understand anything about man. Specifically, one will approve any sort of change in social structures and in the social milieu without consulting the good of man or the improvement of human nature. And one is immured in a relativism in which sociology will seem scientific to the extent that, despite its being an incomplete science in itself, it rejects any insights from the humanistic quarter. Whereas, on the contrary, authentic sociology takes into account both what is developmental and what is damaging for man, and thus it can function in the service of true progress.

If Teilhard de Chardin (a paleontologist, not a sociologist) could depict for us in the noosphere the ideal society of human expansion, it was because he conceived the social vis-à-vis the psychobiological nature of man, and this is not a gift but an aptitude, a vocation, which it is the goal of society to expand and to realize. Man would not be man if his more complex brain were not that of a social being capable of transmitting individual discoveries and of making use of them for the common good. He would be still less man if he were social without his complex brain. He would then be a commonplace social species that would not progress from generation to generation. What has made man is the existence of the super-brain in a social species.

They insist nowadays upon the *socialization* of modern man;

but this is actually only an accentuation of socialization, the forming of a unified humanity throughout the world, the rising importance of Planning vis-à-vis the future in which the role of the State will be greatly stressed. But man was born of successive mutations in the midst of social primates who lived in groups. Since its origin humankind has been distinguished by culture; hence the social dimension, or socialization. One might even say that man was more "social" in the beginning, to the extent that the insufficiency of culture had not allowed him to make his own individuality stand out above the group.

The tragedy of cultural progress is that it has allowed the individual to emerge while social needs have been forgotten in the course of that emergence. And so effectively has this happened that what has appeared is not hyperpersonalization but rather a deviation of personalization, a de-personalization resulting from egoistic individualism. We have forgotten the extent to which we depend upon social education and we think of ourselves as autonomous beings who either through a sense of duty incline charitably toward others, or else reject this duty. We no longer grasp the essential nature of our interdependence and thus have made it a secondary and optional involvement.

It is necessary to re-establish relations between animal sociology (which at this point seems to be a diversion for zoologists) and human society, not so as to confuse them, but because man, however superior he is, is only an instance of a social species, one in which cultural relations remain bio-sociological relations between organisms. As in the matter of consciousness and love, it is necessary to put the discontinuities back into a line of continuity. The animal societies help us to understand the origin of the social fact and its elementary manifestations. Paradoxically one can more readily predict what will result from interrelations between individuals in the insect societies than from those in human societies. One cannot gather men into huge groups, into giant megapolises, without having previously studied the anatomical, physiological, and psychological effects of such grouping, and distinguished the good from the bad.

What animal sociology tells us of the primary social phenomenon is that beings exist who are by nature solitary and have only passing relations—e.g., sexuality and the care of the young—with their kind.

Neither the sexual phenomenon nor the family phenomenon ever succeeds in creating the social phenomenon, which is of another order. A social species is a species whose every individual has inscribed in his flesh and in the instincts of his brain the need of others, and can find individual equilibrium only in a group. The solitary individual is off-balance, he needs others, and he seeks them; and in their absence he is sometimes doomed to die. This is called *affinity* or social *appetition*. According to the level of society, this appetition leads either simply to communal living (sometimes in certain circumstances only), or to mass migrations, or to having a whole succession of communal activities for the purpose of arriving at hierarchical societies provided by different castes (as in the case of insects), or at a simple psychological hierarchy (as in societies of vertebrata).

Animal sociology endeavors to specify more and more clearly for us the mechanism of interactions between individuals which are the automatisms of coordination directing the beneficent progress of society. As always in comparative animal psychology, brain progress leads to a passing from the unconscious to the conscious. This movement is clearly observed when one compares the almost exclusively biological relation between two insects, with the relation of social psychology where the other is known as another, as when one reaches the brain of birds and mammal.

This social affinity is possessed by man; but in man, as always, brain progress works to replace the automatism of instinct through the assuming of control by reflective consciousness. In anything concerning nutrition and sexuality man operates within the preconception of having an instinct like the animal. In anything concerning the social, the preconception is the obverse. In his flesh there is a need for others, but man is not conscious of it and he rejects his social dimension, since he is ignorant of it. It is science rather than morality that must specify for him the extent to which he is in fact socialized.

To the man who ignores others, oppresses them, or lets himself be oppressed by them, bio-sociology offers its essential study, the *neurosociology of human relations* (without the brain man would have no relations). The neurosociological aspect, which is so much misunderstood, should therefore be a testimony, as well as an object of heuristic and prospective researches.

An isolated man is a denaturalized man. The adult, fully developed man may wish for solitude. It is not the same with the human child, who has need of a human social milieu so that his brain may not only function but may also mature normally and completely. The isolated child deprived of culture has positive cerebral deficiencies, notably from the viewpoint of language. There exists a whole gradation in the perversion of desocialized man, ranging from the completely isolated child who becomes an idiot to the "wolf-child" who becomes "wolf-like" by arresting and even by losing his human aptitudes. Thus he is like the deaf person who becomes dumb—but the deafmute's retardation is worse because he lives in a human society and develops the serious disturbances produced by the limitations or the traumata of childhood, such as have been described under the name of *hospitalisme* [2] and those turned up by psychoanalysis.

---

2. A term (not current in English translation) denoting the physical and psychic harm to a small child deprived of affection of the maternal type during a prolonged stay in hospital or custodial institution.—*Ed.*

Thus we can be ourselves only according as the environment of development has orientated our hereditary make-up. There are good, humanizing environments and bad, dehumanizing environments. The environment for man is not the lonely natural environment; it is primarily the human social environment, the source of interhuman emotional and cultural relation. This is also the formative educational environment for freedom and the self-mastery so lacking today.

The opposite of this natural disaster of the "wolf-children" is the experience of total access to our cultural level on the part of young savages separated before the age of five from their environment (after this age the inadequacy of environment would prevent them from retaining their full potentialities—if, of course, the environment was culturally very deficient).

"Wolf-children" may seem very remote from our problems. And yet without going that far one may today see proof of the terrible ravages of isolation. For one thing, this is a leading problem for those engaged in the conquest of the cosmos. Is it possible for anyone to hold out isolated in an environment so far from one's accustomed conditions? We know of the experience of Admiral Byrd alone at the South Pole, or more recently that of Michel Siffre in the French caves. But it is not necessary to go into outer space or down into the depths to be alone. Loneliness is the lot of more and more inhabitants of our cities, where man has the look of a social being desocialized. He is lost in the crowd: either constrained or left to his useless liberty, at the mercy of what is going on at the time. Man, who was made for the human relations of a small community, is finding them less and less in "secular city." And this is accentuated in the case of those who have difficulty entering into relations at best, and especially in the case of women on their own who have no one to love and are loved by no one.

The disturbance of the celibate is not due to chastity, but most frequently to his or her isolation. Marriage only redresses the balance by generating human affection and also certain real human relations that could be obtained as well by re-socialization without marriage and genital relations. To look upon marriage as a panacea is to ignore the considerable number of failures—separations and divorces explained primarily by the fact that no valuable dialogue took place either before or after marriage. The mother of a large family in her own home often, and quite reasonably, feels isolated though surrounded by her own.

The fact is that the social structures of earlier times did impose some sort of social relations, while in the individualism of today, even if socially practiced, it is possible to evade such relations or to reduce them to a quite insufficient minimum. This is not a question of bemoaning the passing of the primitive tribe—and in any case, the personality of modern man would certainly not adapt to its oppressiveness. Nevertheless man did find in the tribe a community environment much more suited to what he needs to keep his balance. It is essential for us today to restore to modern man's life-style conditions that are at least analogically comparable. It should be the normative task of a complete scientific sociology and of a humanist political science to specify these conditions. Yet it fell to Teilhard, a paleontologist, to begin pointing them out to us in the concept of the noosphere he proposes for our implementation.

What is involved is an ideal of society in which the individual and his social needs will finally be reconciled and where personal development will rest upon interpersonal and personalizing relations based on reciprocal love. This is the natural society of man where his nature will be able to flower to the full. But like everything natural, it will be achieved not spontaneously but, rather, by strenuous effort; yet its achievement is an urgent duty if we do not wish to perish for lack of love. Conditions favorable to the achievement of a beneficent socialization that will respect the human person must be established, conditions such as have been spelled out in the encyclical *Mater et Magistra.*

It is, moreover, rather significant that we consider society to be the enemy of the person, preferring liberal, destructive anarchy to totalitarian oppression, which at least has the merit of envisioning a common good to be realized, however wrong in the methods chosen to do so. We seem unaware that the human person is not an isolated individual, but an individual in personal relation with other persons in liberty, equality, and fraternity.

This should help us to understand neurosociology if it existed—and it is only waiting for us to demand it in order to come into existence. It is waiting also for us to agree to put this fundamental question to ourselves: Since there are no social relations when one is in a coma, how does our brain allow us social relations? and, our brain being what it is, what should correct social relations be between human beings?

The neurosociology we envisage should have to develop at all three levels of our cerebral hierarchy. At the level of the *primitive* brain it places the seat of our physical need of others, of our social appetition we have to recognize as an obscure vestige of the social instincts directing the harmony of the social relations of the social animals. We have not only a need for vital expansion driving us toward aggressiveness and domination respecting others (and perhaps leading others to retaliate in kind). These are natural temptations to denaturalize ourselves through pride and humiliation—temptations whose social aspect we shall encounter again after drawing attention to them in a general way in individual psychophysiology.

Competing with this need and modifying it comes the social need of sympathy which limits our aggressiveness as it does among the social animals—with the difference that we must discover this need and consciously assume it instead of being bound as an animal is by his automatism. All this elementary sociability of the primitive brain is, as always, closely related to our affectivity. The correct and balanced relation with the other person is agreeable, and leads us to be agreeable and to seek agreeable beings, to adopt this specifically human behavior of sociability: to *smile* at someone and to receive his smile.

The social drive is the unconscious sense of our limitations and insufficiency, the need to be *completed*. This want is not regulated by simply coexisting; it requires a genuine relation—whether of emotional exchange or of dialogue or of collaboration. It is a consensus on giving and receiving which must develop in a harmonious optimum vis-à-vis the freedom of the other person, and its supreme test is to give oneself and to receive the gift of the other person—which of course requires, for the gift to be valid, that each is truly *existing*. But it is not a matter of possessing, or of taking over, or of allowing oneself to be possessed through self-abdication.

This is inscribed in our bio-sociology all unknown to us. Hence we can be unaware of it and conduct ourselves in directly contrary fashion yet in apparent equilibrium with it. It is only apparent, however, because we are acting in opposition to the profound meaning of our being, as will soon appear in our demeanor, notably in aggressive reactions of dissatisfaction whose true motive we do not understand.

On this elementary, instinctive, infraconscious level the second neurosociological level is erected. For this higher level the *noetic* brain is responsible, the brain that takes cognizance of the other person and of mutual reactions, the brain of social habits. The other person inscribed in our flesh at the instinctual level becomes here an element of our inner depths. The cerebral image of the other person, verbalized in the "you" and the person's name, faces the cerebral image of our ego so important for the consciousness and the will. His reactions are thus inscribed in us in their reality as well as in memory, just as ours are inscribed in his brain.

And finally we must assume all these automatisms of neuro-sociology in full reflective consciousness with the *prefrontal* brain, the brain of love. It is its functional norm that should make us repudiate indifference or hatred and choose the way of love, for this way alone respects the interpersonal relation of two freedoms. Anyone who has a need of others and whose brain is made for assuming his needs by discovering what he must love for a more authentic existence, is obliged to love others in order to love himself properly. Any other attitude is foolishness, disruptive and unhygienic and dangerous to the two people both in relation to one another and as individuals by reason of the social imbalance resulting from it. It is our duty in pursuance of the optimum to *be* fully, to love and to be lovable, to accept the truth that we should be loved and to ask of others a reciprocal lovableness.

Egoism, pathological on the individual plane, is even more so on the social plane; but neither the altruism of self-forgetfulness nor the false egotistical altruism desiring to do good to the other person in spite of himself, has anything to offer by way of a cure for it.

Thus we see how the need for others induces respect for the conditions of their personalization just as they should respect ours, and objectifies for us the necessity of loving one's neighbor with the same love, in the same spirit, and under the same favorable conditions as one loves oneself. It is not easy, but the same techniques of clarity of vision, of self-mastery, and of true willing apply here. The desocialized, isolated person no longer *exists;* he has forgotten his body. He is retrained to exist and to express his existence, but in a way limited by others and in a communal ambience of relations with the teacher and other pupils in which he recovers the power of relating affectively. The Vittoz exercises all train us to accept the other person and his existence by accepting our own. This is not a school for egoism but for resocialization. It is to the extent that we *be-*

come ourselves in the optimum that we feel and reveal ourselves as happy and contented and become lovable and attractive to others.

Let us listen again to Dr. Vittoz:

"Whether we wish it or not, we have an influence in the world for good or bad from the very fact of our interior state, radiating around us peace, energy, joy, generosity—if we possess them, or conversely trouble, discouragement, sadness, and malevolence. Hence it is for us a matter of conscience to induce and to sustain in ourselves those states of soul that are beneficial for others as well as for ourselves. We owe it to our neighbor because we are social beings and because we have, whoever we are, a task to fulfill in this world and a share of responsibility in the good that is done or is not done, and in the evil that is committed. Who will ever know the consequences, harmful or beneficial, of an action or a word, and its far-reaching repercussions in the world? I want my patients to radiate well-being.

"Do not look for perfection in others, but in oneself. One elevates others only to the extent that one elevates oneself. Not only is there evil to be avoided, there is good to be done. It is for us a duty of conscience to ensure that others profit by what we have received. To criticize others is to become evil ourselves. One cannot avoid seeing evil where it exists, but there is no need to savor it. What we must do is to seek the good, to find it out; for it does exist.

"All the good that one has in oneself is not for oneself. The need to give is an awakening of being. If you are not adaptable in certain encounters it is because the ego, which should not count, is taking precedence. One must therefore seek the good one can do and not concern oneself further with the rest. One must always be good; goodness opens hearts, and through the heart one obtains everything. One must open oneself, expand, emerge from self and forget oneself in order to give oneself and to do good. The more one forgets self the more one gives and the more one shines out."

But we should add that one cannot forget oneself except when one has first of all learned to exist fully.

We have seen that the law of balance is to be, to have, and to act in the optimum between the too much and the too little. This is not enough to define the human norm, which involves being together in an authentic relation that accords with the optimum of two existences; in the communion of two loves in which our persons reach the high point of their lives.

Prefrontal love not only ensures our personal unity, it harmonizes and unifies, it personalizes our relations with others. It ensures acting together in a creative collaboration that ignores the meannesses of envy and jealousy and recognizes the insufficiency of the single individual. It socializes our property—and this is not the negation of a limited right of personal property but the healthy use of this property in the service of the common good. One produces not in order to profit from what one has produced but in order to share in the communal production. And our enthusiasm is not an emotion of solitariness but one of solidarity satisfying the secret social needs of our hearts.

Morality is often considered still from the negative standpoint of what is forbidden us so that we may not harm ourselves or others. The important thing seems to be not to do good but to avoid evil, and so we seek to know, without understanding, what is permitted and what is forbidden. True morality, however, defines the conditions of our humanization and of our contribution to the free humanization of others. The virtues must be re-evaluated, for they are the dynamisms of humanization, of achievements of self-realization. The capital virtues—more important to know but more difficult to name and define than the celebrated capital sins—are not trivial little practices for prudent and obedient children pursuing their own little work of personal perfection, but the norm of behavior for anyone interested in growing personally by being an exemplar and a help for others. (On this point, see my book *Vices des vertus et vertus des vices* [Toulouse, 1963]).

But, as we shall see, love of neighbor is not a successive relation with different persons, it is the collective participation in a beloved human work that extends beyond one's own generation and has, in the view of those who see with eyes of faith, eternal dimensions. This is genuine human socialization, a property of humanity. There is, of course, a narrow and static way of loving one's neighbor, but it is incomplete and still suffers from an egotistical aspect. In personal relations with the other, all mankind should be present, for otherwise the other ceases to be loved for himself. But before we discuss this love for a world-to-be-made, we must develop a few reflections upon the terms and conditions of the interhuman relation of love. To the too apparent easiness of love between equals we shall have to contrast—in order to reconcile them—the more obvious difficulties of human relations where inferiorities and superiorities intermingle.

RESPECT

CHAPTER 5

UNIVERSAL LOVE

Species and Individuals

THE MAN WHO loves everybody loves nobody, it is said—and logically enough, it would seem. And if every man is our neighbor who must be loved, we may be in danger of loving the man who is far away more than the man near at hand, the one we have to live with every day and is more difficult to tolerate for that very reason. The example of Jesus, who gave primacy to love, is there to show us that a universal love does not preclude chosen friendships such as He enjoyed with John, Lazarus, or Magdalen.

And this universal love must encompass even our enemies. This is a difficult commandment but most effective, even if we do see only the practical result. For it is very difficult to remain enemies if at least one of the two parties behaves consistently as a friend: this is the best method of causing the other to reflect and of disarming him. In fact we should not have an enemy, and that is what is implied by this commandment of love. The other person may treat me as an enemy; for me to treat him as one must be unthinkable.

All this often appears to be utopian and impracticable, chiefly because we do not believe it. Perhaps it is because we think that our duty of universal love implies that we must be intimate friends with the whole world, including those with whom we do not feel any affinity. It may also be because we find difficulty in separating love of the sinner from the struggle against sin. Can one love exploiters, those responsible, through their ignorance, neglect, or prejudices, for the wretchedness of others? These two objections have no weight. There is absolutely no question of destroying the value of friendship by forcing it to prevail.

We must understand what primarily is implied in loving one's enemy—and everyone may fit somewhere into the enemy category to the extent that he behaves in an inhuman way. Certainly there can be no question of approving, by love, of someone who is committing evil. But it is not human behavior to attempt to stop him from doing evil through our hatred and violence. When confronting an oppressor, we consider it normal to take the side of the oppressed in order to help him to shake off the oppressor. But this is only a small part of our duty of love. The oppressor has a right to our love, too.

Now, what is involved in loving an oppressor is the ability to understand that he has become perverted and is doing evil to himself, too, by being an oppressor. And hence, while we must work for the advancement of the oppressed, we must also work for the "diminution" of the oppressor. Just as there can be no question of liberating the oppressed in spite of himself, but of helping him to liberate himself, so too the oppressor is not to be deprived through violence of what he thinks his right; rather, he must be led to open his eyes and take cognizance of the imbalance in his human relations.

It is utopian, people will say, to want to make love reign among men through education. But isn't it also utopian to think that "righteous" hatred and "righteous" aggression can serve justice? There are innumerable recent examples in all countries and among all parties, to show us the terrible dangers of so-called "righteous" violence. Whereas, psychobiologically speaking, we are so constructed that the way of hatred and violence leads us inexorably to a state of frenzy blinding us to what we are doing and may brutalize us in the end.

Despite this effect we cannot overlook the crime of dehumanization in which the victim of oppression is kept permanently in a state of violence, even if this violence is manifested not overtly but simply in his inability to expand, in the assault upon his dignity and his liberty, in the fact that he is not treated as a man. When the oppressed is led to revolt and violence he is being more human than if he resigns himself to his destruction and that of his family; yet this violence goads him beyond the limit and in its turn dehumanizes him in the opposite sense. The responsibility for this consequence belongs, of course, to the oppressor, though this does not justify the violence even if it explains it.

It is particularly tricky to prevent one person from harming another without introducing force. However important may be the collective aspect of the struggle of the classes in which the oppressed and oppressors are jointly responsible, such struggle is still only one example of inhuman social relations that are the reverse of love. Like everything else that is natural and normal for man, love is a difficult duty, and indifference and hostility are statistically more frequent. But this is because we have not understood that it is absolutely necessary for our balance that love should be *shared;* it is, as we have seen, because we do not reflect, because we have not a clear vision.

The nervous irritability arising out of our defective hygiene changes into aggressiveness against the other person, who is then made the scapegoat for all the dissatisfactions caused by our inadequacies and those of our environment. It is necessary to work for the humanization both of society and of individuals; but a reform at the top is not effective if it is not "in the wind"—that is, if public opinion has not understood the need for it nor demanded it. We have already observed that by learning to be clear-sighted we shall see what is not going rightly around us. It is not a matter of remaking the world by means of a violent revolution, which is always a sign of failure as well as a danger; it is rather a matter of revolutionizing, but legally and without violence. The unfortunate thing is that here again it is difficult to follow the middle way, much easier to play a violent revolutionary, a reformer who reforms nothing, or a conservative who sacralizes injustice.

We are not called upon to impose good, risking the possibility of confusing the good with our own personal opinion. Still it is certain that the good exists and that we must help each one to discover it in freedom.

Actually the solution lies, first of all, in self-knowledge. To develop this leads to miracles of the faith that moves mountains. Social progress carries us inexorably toward love and we can only impede the current. It used to be difficult to interest people in the people of distant countries, because they really were too far away, and we knew nothing of the catastrophes occurring on the other side of the world. Today we know of them immediately and we actually see the unfortunate people suffering. How could one avoid having one's sympathies awakened? The social injustices that wrongly appeared admissible a short while ago are no longer so today. Who today would endure the sight of a child toiling in a mine? What has cut down the forced labor of political deportees in the Soviet Union has been industrial development that has lessened the need for unskilled labor while demanding competent technicians.

Universal love is not a desideratum imposed upon us by moral theology or philosophy; it is the consequence of the way we are constituted. We are made for love because our personality is love from the most elementary level of the attractions and the interdependence of the organic automatisms up to the peak of our reflective consciousness, which was designed to decide clearly what we should love and how we should love so as to be authentic persons. And such persons, as we have just seen, do not think of themselves as autonomous but in personal relation with other persons, an interpersonal relation being necessarily a relation of love. Love is the harmonizing, unifying, integrating element in ourselves as in society.

To love is to recognize that the individual, however important he may be—and he is the element without which nothing would be—is *incomplete:* he needs to enter into relations in order to complete himself by sharing in the constitution of a *higher group.* The individual is not a static being walled up in his own ego; he is a dynamic being who fulfills himself in mutual exchange, who grows in giving and in receiving, who needs both to integrate exterior elements within himself and to share them with others—and who takes delight in these needs of his.

Clear-sighted love can select a hierarchy of needs among those requiring love, for this clarity of vision is not inconsistent with personal tastes. If by definition I must love all men, this should not imply that I must love them with the same love, and it is perfectly legitimate to have special sympathies and good to indulge them. (The opposite, of course, would not hold true, because antipathies must be mastered in order that we may not fail in love) .

Universal love is founded upon the biological affirmation that all men belong to the same species and consequently have among them the social affinity that comprises the potentiality of interpersonal relations at a level considerably higher than the interindividual relation we can have with a domestic animal—emotion-filled though this too can be. The relation of animal to man is never situated at the human level, but it is the more valuable according as the animal is cerebrally closer to us, as is the case with mammals and to a lesser degree with birds. There really is a certain mutual comprehension, a love between two chosen beings, even if it is not at the human level. One recognizes there the degree of love to which animals, according to their zoological level, may attain.

While the love of brute creation should not be exaggerated to the extent that it leads to a selfish neglect of humankind, still it is good for man to have friendly contacts with the animals with which he is interdependent, since he is born of the biological evolution to which they witness. Man as a living being was not made for a universe of robots where there would be no more animals. He should not treat animals as machines any more than as gods or as slaves. A middle way is to be found, one that definitely allows man to make use of animals, provided that he does not make them suffer.

We should love all animals, but we will have a particular love for one special animal. It is difficult to explain the choices of love. But it is expressed in the fact that animals, like men, are different, and this difference is maximal in man because his personality is maximally developed. It would be difficult to love a fish for itself, for it resembles all other fish. Whereas a certain dog or cat, with its more marked individuality, does not in the least resemble any other dog or cat.

To love someone is to distinguish him. This seems paradoxical. We must love all men because we are all alike, but we must not confuse a loving communion with identification. We must love our neighbor as ourselves precisely because, although he is a man like us, he is different from us. And it is this difference that we must respect because it is this that makes him lovable to us. It is this difference that we need in order to complete us. This makes the dialogue more difficult, but in identity there would be no dialogue, and it is dialogue that we need.

In the predicament of accepting what seems contradictory we either cling to the specific unity of men and are tempted to deny their diversity, or on the contrary we put accent on the diversity and tend to deny the unity. It is to the credit of Existentialism that it has insisted on the originality of each individual as something to be respected—but at the expense of overlooking that it is always a question of the individual manner of being a man.

It is a serious mistake to impede the development of individuality by striving through education to avoid differences; but neither is it right to push our liberalism so far as to accept evil and pathological behavior as free individual options. The good of individuals is contained within the common good.

Biology helps us understand what is meant by the species and what by the individual. The species is what the different individuals have in common. Anthropological analysis explains to us what is specifically human, the characteristics of large groups, and the individual differences. The mechanisms of human reproduction have as their aim both the continuance of the species and the differentiation of the individuals. The study of heredity is the study of the mechanisms that differentiate us from our parents by an entirely new genetic association. To produce a girl-child by parthenogenesis of their mothers without masculine intervention (as will one day be possible) would be biologically bad because the daughter would resemble her mother as would a shoot or a cutting, and this would deprive

humanity of its richness, of the sense of renewal of the generations which the death of individuals turns to the benefit of the
species. Cross-breeding by the union of different individuals is
biologically excellent; whereas, on the contrary, excessive con-
sanguinity is dangerous, as it results in the emergence of blem-
ishes that would otherwise remain hidden, thanks to the genetic
mechanism of dominance and recessiveness.

Those who rightly give precedence to equality among
men—the basis of the struggle against social injustices preventing men from realizing their potentialities—have a tendency to
deviate toward an egalitarianism of leveling that denies individual differences. One might, by means of questionable eugen-
ics (happily outside our competence at present), achieve a
middle type that would eliminate both the least endowed and
the most richly endowed. This would be a grave human perversion. Differences should be recognized; but that is not to deny
the resemblances. Let us be slow to speak of superiority or of
inferiority *per se* among normal individuals, for one is generally inferior or superior in one domain and not in all, and it
would be a mistake to consider only intellectual superiority as
important: there are many other superiorities.

What is most injurious of all is to deny a *human* nature to
the other person; that is what makes the racist. Whatever may
be the apparent superiorities or inferiorities (concerning which
we cannot say whether they come from the hereditary nature of
the individual or from the cultural environment in which he
grew up), it must be stated that all men are to be respected
alike, as persons with whom we must have personal relations in
equality. Love of neighbor is just this, and not some paternalistic type of charity typical rather of the superior protector of his
inferior protégé.

The whole difficulty derives from the word *equal,* which we
confuse with the word *identical,* when in fact men are equals in
their *difference.* They are all human persons having a right to

the same consideration, to the same potentialities for fully and freely realizing their tastes and their aptitudes—a realization not allowed by modern society because of educational differences, whence derive our social or cultural distinctions. But this in no way sanctions the identifying of situations, suppressing the obligation to command and to obey, denying the inferiorities or superiorities, standardizing life in a bureaucratic socialism that kills off individual initiative.

Being equals in difference implies equality in *complementarity*. We have here a "loaded" word, and we must not dissociate it from equality. We need complementarity so as to be completed, but only on condition that we do not make the other person into a small complement who adds his idiosyncrasy to the superior norm we represent. It is contrary to the human meaning of complementarity to express it in terms of superiority and inferiority. True complementarity on the other hand admits of re-establishing interpersonal equality between the person who is in a situation of superiority and a person who is in a situation of inferiority. The one does not give all, nor does the other receive all; it is up to me to recognize the domain in which the other, whoever he may be, is superior to me and I inferior to him. Thus I shall understand that at my level he is a human person with whom it is in my interest to enter into relation, not only to give but also to receive.

To love the other person as oneself is to want to work mutually for his personal expansion, which is to want him to develop freely but in his own fashion and not in ours.

Friendship

These differences among men inspire the different attitudes we adopt upon entering into relations with them. The love we bear toward others must affect all men but in differing terms and conditions that are difficult to express in words.

Just before his death, Father Lepp brought the weight of his experience as a psychologist to bear upon "the ways of friendship," and we refer the reader to his book of that title (New York, 1966). We shall only recall that if love is universal, *friendship* is of necessity "particular": a selective relation between two persons with its own emotional intensity, quite distinct from comradeship or from love interpreted in the restricted sense concerned with the elective choice of a man and woman making up a married couple.

Friendship has its own special characteristics, seen at their best in cases where friends have no other reason for meeting except their friendship. Friendship may exist between comrades or between neighbors, but it does not demand comradeship or proximity or the existence of common interests, for it is an *affinity of souls*. As the superpersonalization of universal love for all men, friendship can serve to express a particular type of relation between husband and wife as a couple, or of family relations between parents and children, or brothers and sisters who are bound not only by conjugal or family links but also by a kind of free choice and a more particular affinity. But friendship does not take the place here of the conjugal or the family relation; it simply gives it a supplementary aspect. Brothers who are friends are not ordinary friends. The father who is a friend must remain a father. And to say that brothers can be friends as well as being brothers, or that a father can also be a friend, does not imply that they have to be so. What they have to do is practice a true fraternal or paternal love to which friendship is added.

What about the couple? It is a mistake to equate friendship with conjugal love because it becomes continent, say, in old age. Conjugal love consists in more than sexual relations; it is the communion between two people that forms the *couple* and is a particular modality of human relations based upon one type of love. Such a love will never transform itself into a friendship.

And if in its origins it had been primarily a friendship, a total mutation is called for to lead to that love without which the couple would not be a true couple.

What transforms friendship into love, or what reveals love, is not sexual attraction, it is the desire to live life entirely together by forming a *couple* that will become a *family*. But within the framework of conjugal love there can be nuances, and it is correct to say that there are couples who are in addition truly friends without that friendship's replacing love or being essential to it. This added friendship facilitates the dialogue but does not imply that in its absence conjugal love will exclude dialogue.

Since we are what we are, we must love all men; and this does not mean that we are to feel a vague love for humanity having no existence of its own outside individuals, but that we must love men themselves. And these men are to be loved in all the characteristics of their personality—that is, in their cultural, social, and religious characteristics. We must love the Chinese as a Chinese, the Buddhist in his Buddhism, the Communist in his Communism. And this is the basis of the ecumenical dialogue of cultures and of religions in which each gives to the other and receives from him, working toward his development and not his conversion—or rather, each knowing that such development is leading to a convergence that is not a betrayal. But this love for far-away people with whom contact is difficult will be exercised principally through the medium of social institutions that permit the progress of humanity. In these days of extended leisure it could include the duty of traveling for the sake of entering into rapport, or of receiving strangers into one's home.

But if in all our encounters we must be lovable in order to love and be loved, if we must be open to the mystery of affinities that may perhaps be revealed in the course of the encounter, it is still true that this is quite different from the more selective levels of love our personalities also have need of. We have need of the love that is found in the collaboration of comradeship born of propinquity whether in our professional work or in our housing set-up. We must love specially, according to this more particular set of conditions, those nearest and those with whom we should join in fellowship. But this is not to imply that comradeship is friendship. We have an equal need for the greater intimacy of friendship, and altruism and comradeship do not take its place. The adolescent's personality has special need of it; and, as Lepp demonstrates so well, panic at the thought of "particular friendship" in the pejorative sense must not be allowed to hinder its expansion. There ought to be vigilance, but not an excessive or hurtful prudence. We know only too well how single women can become unbalanced by living alone so as to avoid the slander of those for whom female friendships are always tinged with guilt.

We won't dwell here on the complications added to friendship and simple social love by sexual difference, since we shall be returning to this when we come to define the ambiguous connections between love and sexuality. We know how the possibility of friendship between man and woman has been a point at issue because of the risk of its becoming a carnal adventure—sometimes without love. That there is a risk is certain because of our ignorance of what sex fully is, but this in no way implies the impossibility of such a friendship. It only requires a special prudence and, of course, a still greater prudence if each is married. But in this case it will not be possible for the friendship to be confined to the two persons: it will necessarily have to allow also for the other commitments of each of the two. It is normal for a friend of one of the children to be accepted in the family; and both the male and the female friends of husband and wife must be considered as friends of the couple—that is, as having a special relation with the other partner, who cannot be a stranger to them.

Comradeship, friendship, conjugal or family love are more intense variations of human love, a special relation between two people who have chosen each other or whom life has brought together; these relations do not conflict with the law of loving all men. There is here no sort of closed-in egoism for two, for the two—or more than two—people concerned love all others. We must break the pernicious habit of considering ourselves as isolated individuals, and look upon ourselves and others in their individuality, certainly, but always as members of the human community whether under its proximate or more remote aspect.

CHAPTER 6

COUNSELING AND LOVE

The Model of Competence

LOVE AMONG HUMAN BEINGS is possible only in the recognition—beneath their diversities and their situational inequalities in aptitudes, tastes, even courage—of their equality as human personalities. To assert oneself or to accept oneself as being by nature inferior or superior betrays a disturbed attitude that prevents one from loving himself or his neighbor in the right way. I must recognize my adequacies and my inadequacies, recognize that the other person is a human being like myself, and that our differences are caused by the accidents of heredity and of education for which neither of us is responsible and which carry with them neither merit nor demerit.

Nonetheless, while there are pseudo-superiorities and pseudo-inferiorities attaching especially to appearances and situations, there are genuine superiorities that we must recognize and know how to handle. But in this case it is still possible to have a balanced human relation, which is of course a relation of social love, of sympathy, one that the relation of obedience—even when the obedience is mixed with admiration—cannot take the place of between the two individuals concerned. How can the interpersonal balance be maintained in a relation where the one in a prescriptive position of authority gives more than the other who comes to receive, who has a prescriptive right to receive?

Such relations are encountered every day. First of all, the relation between a child and its parents, between child and adult, between child and educators, is at the base of every personality. This relation is found again between the adult who needs advice and the one he goes to get it from by reason of his competence to give it: the patient and doctor, the individual in difficulty and the professional adviser in his particular field, master and disciple, professional or civil superior and his subordinate, poor and rich ranged in class struggle, peoples of superior culture and of inferior culture in dialogue. We must help other people to develop in the freedom of their own initiative and without crushing them beneath the weight of our competence. We must see to it that this same competence—indisputable and beneficial as it may be—does not unbalance us by isolating us in superiority and so get between us and authentic human relations.

There have to be counselors, preceptors, models. But such counselors, such preceptors and models should neither consider themselves primarily nor be considered primarily in terms of technical competence but rather as men with their own difficulties, their own problems and cares that will bring them back again to the level of ordinary humanity. A model does not have to be a paragon of perfection but simply one who thoroughly grasps where perfection lies (ordinarily in a specific field) and is trained in the methods of attaining it. It is better that he have the experience of applying these methods himself and of succeeding at it for this will increase his competence and the confidence placed in him. (On the other hand, the instructive experience of failure may qualify him better than never to have known failure at all.) The main thing is the valuable counsel he gives.

But the significance of such counsel must be understood. We are not about to buy an infallible recipe from a magician, a recipe that will save us in spite of ourselves and without our participation (*ex opere operato,* so to speak.—*Ed.*) . The specialist teaches us what we must do; he requires our participation by explaining so that we can understand and by encouraging us to a personal effort. He cannot put himself entirely in his client's place, and, above all, he cannot take the initiative away from him. He is called upon simply to enlighten him so that he may decide with full knowledge of the facts, not in order to please or as a matter of obedience, but because he has understood the necessity and the advantage of what he is doing.

Counseling is all the more difficult because it is necessary to have understood the situation, always complex and, generally speaking, one bringing into play various persons who in all good faith proffer contradictory aspects of the truth. Secondly, one must leave the individual free to make his decision without imposing it on him, and yet at the same time suggest to him how to go about seeking the truth. To put it in technical terms, a counselor ought to be "non-directive" but at the same time to have a sufficient amount of directivity to enable the individual to reach the stage of correcting his mistakes.

While it used to be necessary to insist upon the non-directive approach—and this often remains true still—we must not forget the reverse tendency, which would allow everyone, in its denial of a moral absolute, to do as he pleases from the time he can think. We must not altogether confuse counseling with psychoanalytical technique. In analysis the goal is not moral formation but simply to free one from neurotic complexes by bringing to light situations from the past which were causing the conflict and are the true hidden cause of the present behavioral trouble. By his very presence the psychoanalyst leads the patient to recover his freedom, but it is not his role to teach him that his liberty is not license to do anything at all he likes. The counselor, on the other hand, cannot restrict himself to inducing relaxation in the course of the confidential dialogue; he must also indicate what to do.

What is common to the psychoanalyst and the bona fide counselor is the human relation established between the specialist and the patient. This is what psychoanalysis has brought to light under the technical name of transference and countertransference. These are the professional modalities of emotional relations, of social love; and they throw considerable light on the mechanisms of interpersonal relations (see A. L. M. Hesnard, *Psychanalyse du lien interhumain* [Paris, 1957]) .

The specialist is not only a specialist, he is also a man; and it is a man the patient, behind the apparent motivation of resolving his problems, is unconsciously seeking, with the deep-rooted purpose of contacting a man as a man, of engaging him, of obtaining his love and his protection—both of which relations are, generally speaking, lacking in his own life. And the specialist who thinks of himself on the technical plane acts in reality as much by his presence, by that which he consciously and unconsciously is, as by what he prescribes.

Dr. Michael Balint's recent studies have thrown fresh light

upon the problem of the patient-physician relation by helping us to understand the effectiveness of unqualified healers who sometimes do better than qualified doctors.[1]

When it abandons the approach of the old family doctor who was always his patient's friend, scientific medicine becomes a specialized discipline that knows only ailing organs, symptoms, illnesses, and threatens to forget the patient himself. The old human relation of doctor and patient looked like a kind of social convention causing precious time to be pointlessly lost, and the doctor might almost have wished he were a veterinary surgeon, or caring only for unconscious patients.

Today we realize that an essential part in therapeutic effectiveness is played by the doctor serving as a medicine. The doctor does not cure solely by what he gives, but by what he is and by what he says. The human relation through emotion or dialogue is either stabilizing or unbalancing; it cannot be neutral. It is psychotherapy; and while psychotherapy in the technical sense concerns mental patients and requires specialization, every man has a need of it and receives it automatically from others, in the same way as, without even wishing to, he exercises it upon others. Let us try consciously to be beneficial "drugs" by knowing how to be and how to *love*. Balance in the normal person is an effort of dynamic counterpoise that is not easy to achieve.

There was a time—which unfortunately is not entirely past—when the first aim of medical diagnosis was to distinguish the genuine patient, one with organic trouble, from the "phony" patient who was simply one with "nerves" and whose functional troubles were only imaginary. The first needed treatment, the other could be cured with suggestion.

---

1. The author's reference, J. P. Valabrega's *La Relation thérapeutique,* is not available in English, but Dr. Balint's work, *The Doctor, His Patient, and the Illness* (New York, 1957), was translated from English by Dr. Valabrega.—*Ed.*

Now obviously it is paradoxical to deny that "nerves" exists when one knows that nervous disorder is sending impulses through all the organs so disturbing that eventually a burning sensation in the stomach, caused by the imagination but very real for all, that can end up in an ulcer. Let us stop claiming the unreality of the imaginary, for it is nonexistent only so far as external reality is concerned but perfectly real in our brain. To imagine is to give to what is unreal a cerebral reality that makes it an active factor in the system. Imagination often plays upon the bad; we must utilize it for the good by becoming calm in ourselves and by helping others to calm themselves by our influence.

In the agitated and anguished world of today, the prey to nervous fatigue, it is the nervous who become the principal invalids, so much so in fact that they succumb to maladies of civilization like coronary thrombosis.

It is unthinkable for the responsible specialist to care for an organ independently of the patient's psychism and life conditions that are sending this organ nervous, disturbing messages and thereby sustaining the illness and retarding recovery. Hence he must add to all the medical treatment a psychotherapy usually taking the form of simple confidence and reassuring explanation. Conversely, in order to reinforce this attitude, the doctor must bear in mind as well that every organ, whether diseased or only disturbed in its functioning, is sending upsetting messages to the nerve centers by means of the blood and the sensitive nerves. Consequently the patient cannot be in a normal condition of nervous equilibrium, and the doctor must not overlook the fact that his very situation as a patient is necessarily causing him further anxieties. In the relation with his physician the patient is in a state of inferiority, and even more intensively so if he is awaiting diagnosis and cure from the other.

Two agents are operative in illness. There is the direct action of the pathogenic factor on the system, and the system's *reaction*, which will depend on one's health, on one's resistance, on what is called the "terrain," and will condition the variable individual resistance and the disposition to recovery. The microbe and the terrain have all too often been placed in opposite camps. Those who scientifically and objectively emphasized the microbe did not want to allow for the terrain, while conversely those who overestimated the terrain ignored the microbe.

Tuberculosis is certainly caused by the tubercle microbe, but the microbe is not the full story. Everything depends upon our resistance, which is where our hereditary constitution intervenes, and upon our state of health, in which anxiety plays a tremendously important part. Thus the nervous factor is primordial in tuberculosis. An unconscious conflict may resolve itself by a lessening of resistance, thus permitting refuge in genuine illness which cannot be cured, despite remedies, while this conflict remains unresolved. On the other hand tuberculosis, like the treatments for it, has repercussions both biological and psychological on the nervous balance. This is a primordial factor that the sanatorium cannot neglect.

We know today that an important part of successful medical treatment is that of suggestion. On the one hand the system becomes accustomed to react to a treatment so that as physically its effectiveness lessens, psychologically its effectiveness increases. To give a hypnotic pill habitually causes the pill itself, through its shape and colour, to be sufficient to induce sleep. An animal to whom an injection of insulin has been given on many occasions to lower the sugar content of its blood, produces the desired reaction after a simple prick or injection of distilled water.

With man there is no need to go that far: his imagination is enough to ensure its efficacy. Today the same effect is therapeutically produced, for instance, in sleep cures where poisoning of the system is diminished by suppressing a certain number of active medicines, which are replaced, unknown to the patient, by inactive ones. In order to ascertain the imaginary share in the effectiveness of a certain medicine it is replaced, either unknown to the patient alone or unknown to the doctor as well, by an inactive *placebo* (double blind test).

Hence we can see that the word "nervous" does not stand for something without reality but rather for something with a twofold reality. There is the influence of the inferior brain, which is the regulator of organic and cerebral balance and the seat of emotional reactivity, and of the superior brain, seat of the psyche and of the imagination. This is not to oppose a materialistic biological therapy to a psychotherapy that would not be materialistic. The other person is a medicine because through his presence and his words he becomes a cerebral structure within the brain of his interlocutor, and he will calm or agitate the regulator centers at the base of the brain and through them act upon the whole organism. Nothing is more materially real than either the beneficial effect of the drug's confidence and love or the harmful effect of mistrust, hatred, or indifference.

But there are two degrees within this efficacy. There is the blind confidence of one who abandons himself to a specialist to be treated without explanations. Such a one is, to a lesser degree, as passive as the hypnotized person in the hands of the hypnotist. Man being what he is, this passive form of psychotherapy is the least beneficial. The participation of the sick person should be obtained for his recovery. There is a world of difference between two psychological techniques for the suppression of pain in a confinement. A woman may be hypnotized and so, through loss of consciousness, experience no pain. It is distinctly preferable, however, that she spare herself the suffering, not by means of some suggestion that she will not suffer but by reason of an increased awareness and will power. In other words, she knows that the confinement will be less painful to the extent that she does properly everything that is indicated by the way she is feeling.

As the inequality between the adviser in a position of superiority and the sick person in a position of inferiority is prejudicial to proper balance, it is necessary to expend effort in order to lessen it. It is to be hoped that the patient may grow increasingly competent to understand the doctor's explanations and to take part in his own cure. People are not cured; they are helped to cure themselves. But to achieve this, real education is required, and not that type of superficial journalistic information that makes a sick person demanding the latest pill impossible to care for. He considers himself competent to know what is best for him, whereas the true competence that would flow from the self-knowledge he lacks would help him to realize that the doctor is more competent than he.

It would certainly be much more convenient for the specialist to give his full attention to his patient, unhampered by the human factor, without becoming personally concerned with what makes his patient "people"; but human relations being what they are, he could do so only at the risk of precipitating new disorders. Here, too, we are obliged to love our neighbor correctly as ourselves. While there is a great deal to be reformed in medicine, in this respect it would not be at all desirable that progress should come about through increased anonymous bureaucracy that would suppress this human factor.

But what is true of patient-physician relations is just as true of all human relations. We are all of us medicines for one another. In our relations with the other person our anxieties and his counteract each other. Let us be aware of this so that we may not do harm by believing in an impossible objectivity. And the most important element in what we are, as modern psychology has demonstrated so well, is not the outward appearances, or the declared intentions, but what is behind all this and derives from the unconscious.

Why are we so irritated, so aggressive? It is not because the other person has provoked it but because we are tired, nervously exhausted, that we resolve our unconscious difficulties by an aggressive attack upon another, quite innocent person. One who is imbalanced by pride or is made so by someone else as the result of humiliation could not have a normal reactivity. He will counterbalance the inhuman situation in which he finds himself by an aggressiveness expressing in one case his need to establish himself by emerging from his humiliation, and in the other the necessity of humiliating the other person by trying to justify his false superiority.

Every human relation is a mutual collaboration toward humanization. Two factors contributing to the effectiveness of the encounter and of the dialogue have to be reckoned with: *human* value, and competence, which go hand in hand. Neither the counselor nor the counseled should forget that they are human persons, not slaves, tyrants, or gods. There is never a superior and inferior except on the technical plane, but if this plane is severed from the human plane then the competent technician becomes a technocrat whose competence loses its human value. Nothing is more difficult than to ask help or advice without becoming diminished; nothing is more difficult than to give help or advice without becoming excessively self-important.

The person who is consulted for his technological knowledge should never forget that he is a man, weak and fragile like all men; and the person who comes to consult him should not put him on a pedestal. His superiority lies only in his professional qualifications, and exists fully only if that competence is grafted on to a true human superiority that, as we have seen, belongs to the category of the heart. "Poor among the poor" should be the slogan of the technician—that is to say, a man among men; whereas his competence has a tendency to make him rich, aloof, and therefore dehumanized, as one who can no longer be himself in the truth of his love, since love demands a relation of equality in complementarity.

Nothing is more prejudicial to human equilibrium than this spurious superiority of the technician who despises ordinary people often under cover of a false paternalistic charity. On the plea that they have not our education—poor though it is in humanizing qualities, as we have seen—the needy are considered incapable of genuine effort as if they were not really men. Christianity is not a skin-deep religion. For that very reason it has never been presented as an esoteric cult for the satisfaction of an elite as was, for example, Albigensian Catharism, which distinguished the "perfect" from the ordinary people. Right from the beginning it has been the religion of the poor. St. Paul was rejected by the intellectuals of Athens, who laughed at him, but listened to by the dockers of Corinth. They were the real elite, because they were people of heart.

The best example of this may be seen in the sphere of birth regulation. Here the technocrats unhesitatingly recommend the worst, most harmful processes, from the standpoint not only of love but also of hygiene and mental health, simply because they consider self-control impossible for the masses and they decline to educate them to that end. This real though pseudo-charitable racism of the technocrats, mating, drugging, and mutilating human beings as though they were beasts, and all ostensibly for their own good, must be counteracted by the true charity of true human technicians who do not hesitate to become educators in love, for they truly believe in man. Unfortunately the "charitable" proclamations of Catholics who espouse contraception make more noise in the world than the wonderful educative experiences of marriage counselors in our Western countries and even in underdeveloped areas. How many have so much as heard of the magnificent apostolate of the doctors Guy on the Island of Mauritius?

This is only one example of what can be obtained when two

men "dialogue" in equality in the course of their search for the truth. But unfortunately the modern technician cares very little about the truth and is interested only in efficiency. One day he may understand that *love alone is efficient*—on condition that it enters into partnership with technical competence. This is the tragedy of the patient who receives emotional support from an unqualified healer rather than a qualified physician. With the suppression of the healers, their role should be taken over by the physicians. But possibly modern man is too dependent on healers. Perhaps while we are denouncing the technocrat's inhumanity we should denounce as well modern man's surrender to the all-powerful magician who is expected to relieve him of all effort. What belongs to the healer should not be relinquished completely to the doctor in order to make him into a kind of super-sorcerer; it should be given back to the patient, for he is the one who, with the help of the doctor, should become his own healer, not by letting himself become suggestible, but by understanding, and so getting over his apprehensions.

Since all men are different, men are superior in some aspects and inferior in others. The person who lives in a state of human balance because he knows how to love properly is able to bring to the most deprived person the knowledge of his superiority, and to the proudest person the knowledge of his inferiority. In a state of equality-identity, the just hierarchy allowing of the harmonious achievement of human tasks would be impossible. In the matter of a difference of functions, which ought to be related as far as possible to aptitudes, there must be some people who command and others who obey. But the commanding and the obeying must remain within the framework of human relations.

One person is not made to obey and another to command in all matters and at all times throughout their lives. The one who is commanding is not infallible and all-powerful; he must not impose but rather convince, in a human dialogue that fully allows for the point of view of the other, who is not a slave but a collaborator. And the one who is obeying obeys in a healthy fashion only when he has understood—that is, when he has made his own the order he received so that in obeying the other he is obeying himself. Nothing is more difficult than to command and to obey in sane and healthy fashion, but we cannot abandon the attempt without rousing serious disturbances in the form of the neurotic pride of the tyrant and the neurotic humiliation of the slave, and this is expressed in their dis-satisfaction, their neurosis, and their aggressiveness.

Thus in all areas and at all times we are practicing human relations within some situation of inequality, whether it concerns counsel sought or given, or professional problems, political authority, or family decisions. The point is that this inequality should become something enriching, instead of being, as it nearly always is today, a source of imbalance and *ressentiment*.

Helping in Growth

If inequality of situation, of competence, and of wealth is an unbalancing factor, how much more so is the natural inequality arising from the difference between adults and young people. A young person must always remain someone who has not yet reached full growth or attained his full potentialities, while the adult, by definition, has attained this fulfillment. The duty of the adult—and more especially that of parents and educators—is to educate the young person, to exercise a certain amount of authority over him in order to help him to become truly adult.

A healthy education demands an interpersonal relation that is effective—i.e., stabilizing. If the adult turns the young person into a slave who must obey him without understanding, if education turns into a sort of animal training, it is not formative but rather a source of neurotic repression, and will never produce a free, responsible adult. By way of avoiding this classic catastrophe, which today is unacceptable within the context of the right to liberty, we fall into the opposite excess of imposing no authority whatsoever. The young person is left to push his way up like a mushroom, to "live it up" during his youth, and thus he is rendered incapable of being a free and responsible person. People who thus exercise either excessive or insufficient authority do not know how to love; and so they help to form human beings incapable of loving.

Parents and educators must maintain relations that respect the personality of every young person, while at the same time recognizing that each one is in the course of formation and that they themselves have a role to play in that formation. Young people need a certain amount of authority and suffer from lack of it; but it must be a human authority. Parents and educators are not tyrants, but they are not "pals" either. They should manage to be friends without dropping the difference between the adult and the non-adult or denying the character of educator or of father or mother. As in every other relation, they must be able to love because they have fully understood what love means. The emotional component, so important in education since emotional difficulty can block its progress, is not added on as a tedious complication; it is essential to the educative relation, provided that it is controlled and does not degenerate into unstabilizing sentimentality. There are no authentic human relations without reciprocal love.

So while the difference between adult and young must not be minimized, yet at the same time it ought not to be exaggerated to the extent of denying the personal dimension of the young, who right from the beginning should be looked upon as future persons who must be made ready for freedom, and not animals to be trained. Even the infant is a little person who has a need of love, but it does not follow that he must bend everyone around him to his whim; he must be led without excessive coercion to adopt as his rule the standard of adults. The child was not made just to obey without further ado; he should understand the reasons for his obedience so that he may learn freely to obey commands that are good.

Our practice has turned up two states that exist side by side. There is the (chronological) adult who gives orders and counsels that are often in obvious contradiction to what he is and does, or with what adults are and do. And there is the young person who is waiting desperately for the moment when he too will be an adult and free to act according to his own choice without being forced to obey any longer. An adult who is incapable of self-control obviously cannot teach it to a young person, who is even less capable of it than he himself. We should restore the truth of the continuity of the vital cycle. No one has reached adulthood; everyone is moving toward it. Some are far along; others are in the earlier stages. The normal adult state bespeaks a certain achievement that yields greater opportunities for mastery, provided, of course, that a good education has made it possible. When adults behave badly it is precisely because they are not adult, since no one has taught them to be so. Instead of waiting for the moment to be able to imitate such adults, young people ought to take the opposite approach and become truly free adults, and not infantile "adults" who constitute the majority of men.

Nonetheless, adulthood is not a static condition of perfection and balance. All his life man will have to struggle to climb, to realize himself more fully, to mature, to grow continually more adult; otherwise he is certain to deteriorate. The model adult is not one who can glibly produce the false, facile, depressing virtue for someone who is in a difficulty. The model adult is someone who knows where the good lies and who endeavors, despite his failures, to climb always toward it. By expecting an effort of the young person the adult will thereby show him not only what the adult condition is but also that it is the human condition to the very end of life.

The young person, for his part, must understand the *positive* necessity for this effort. He must be led to realize that effort is the essential condition for being a true man, and not a man of conformity or legalism. All too often he is simply forbidden to do what "isn't done" and commanded to do what *is* done without ever being told the point of such action: that he is responding to the necessity for human improvement and the realization of human potentialities. The young person understands very well the tough asceticism involved in training for athletics and sports. He should be helped to understand that the same asceticism is necessary in order to become a man—i.e., a free being. Constraints are not imposed upon him simply because he is young. He is being offered a technique for learning how to use his brain to become a fully human, adult, normal, civilized man, and not a stunted personality.

Every stage in the formation of a real human being—that is, of someone capable of loving correctly—is important. Early infancy is the source of the basic consciousness, and is normal only when the child has been surrounded by authentic love, that is, the happy medium between lack of love and false love (which makes an idol of him) ; and when he has been able to find correct human models around him—models of love, not because of what they say but because of what (unconsciously and consciously) they are and what they do. Then comes childhood with its elementary formation in self-control and initiation into the human condition.

But doubtless the most important stage is adolescence, a period of shifting between the genital maturity of puberty and the adult state: a typically human period not experienced by any animal. It is because people do not understand its significance that there are so few real adults on the level of self-mastery—that is, with the *aptitude* to love. People see in the adolescent a sort of pre-adult who ought still to be obeying when he is in fact revolting. The revolt is legitimate if he is being constrained in the name of a negative morality; but it is catastrophic insofar as it keeps him from completing his psychological growth.

Constraining an adolescent, or, conversely, letting him do whatever he likes, amounts to preventing him from growing up. Psychological maturation entails an asceticism of struggle against egoism, and an openness to other people which, for all that it is the normal and natural tendency to maturation, is nevertheless a difficult discipline, and easy to fail in. Anyone who habitually lets himself go in matters of sensuality and "phony" sentimentality is in danger of never becoming truly adult, for he will be immured in his own egoism. Yet one does not gain altruism by prohibiting egoism. Egoism remains as a forbidden temptation at the center of the personality—the normal thing if not forbidden by the moralist. Nor is this prohibition an arbitrary and provisional one that will cease to apply once we are adult; it is the very law of our being which we must learn to apply.

We must learn the law of love that composes us, and that by developing the clarity of vision to understand it in ourselves and to maintain with other persons of both sexes authentic relations that are indispensable to reciprocal growth. Adolescence is a crucial period of human life, for it is at this time that we acquire all the bad habits that will hinder us from being authentically adult. If the human world is an absurd hell, this is simply because it is peopled by men of prolonged adolescence who are either indulging their egoism or repressing egoism for moral reasons. Nothing is more pitiable than these crumbling, frustrated people who are doing harm without realizing it, without even being capable of responsibility for the harm they do. They are not deserving of everlasting hell but rather of some celestial mental hospital where they will be admitted out of pity for their frustration.

There is a solemnness to adolescence because it is then the decision for the whole future is taken; and the adolescent should be helped in reaching this decision. At best this is *normally difficult* because of the generation gap; but it will certainly be less difficult if we have understood the difficulty of human relations in general, the difficulty of being human, the difficulty of being able to love. The good educator is not one who has no problems at all, but who, though he has problems and is therefore in the same league as other people, understands better than they what has to be done about them.

While it is unintelligent not to grasp the seriousness of the adolescent crisis, which is the overture toward adult love and liberty, it is just as serious a presumption to think that there are irreversible, hopeless failures. To be sure, it is better not to have to correct deviations and bad habits. But it is never too late to learn how to love, and to work at becoming an authentic man.

The Human Mosaic

The basis of all authentic human relation is reciprocal esteem; contempt, even if it grows out of pity, vitiates this relation. For one thing, every man is worthy of esteem. When we are confronted by the obvious and inevitable differences between men, we have a tendency toward either contempt or envy for whatever is different from us. We tend to think ourselves superior, for we are very well aware of the imbalance resulting from recognizing an inferior nature in ourselves; but we are not aware of the corresponding harmfulness of considering ourselves to be of a superior nature. Anyone who thinks himself superior despises inferiors who have not his capacities, and is jealous of superiors whose superiority he does not recognize, yet whom he envies as enjoying undeserved success.

This error of thinking oneself naturally superior is the feature of racism that corrupts the relations between men of differing civilizations. But the racist attitude is only one particular aspect affecting our relations with those of a differing physical type or culture. In fact it is pure racism that dominates the struggle of all the human groups that consider themselves not as different and complementary in equality but as superiors confronting inferiors: men and women, rich and poor, intellectuals and laborers, primitive and cultured, provincials and cosmopolitans, peasants and citizens, professionals and nonprofessionals, adults and young people. We decide that this being who is strange because he is not like us is not a true human person, that he is of a different nature and that he has not the same rights since he has not the same aptitudes. We give an absolute value to contingent things such as skin coloration, social customs, or life situation. Instead of seeing injustices in situations that involve alleged inferiority, we justify them as being inevitable because they are founded in nature.

This is a serious error, one we should drop in favor of an accurate concept of the human nature common to all men, of their equal potentialities under individual variants. We are wholly mistaken when we attribute some inferiority to a physical type; this is racism in the narrow sense of the word. Human inferiorities and superiorities derive from lesser or greater humanizing elements in the cultural milieu. But it would still be racism (the racism of many anti-racists) to put a higher value on our culture by treating others as savages who have a claim to our culture as being the only civilized culture. There are in fact no inferior or superior cultures, but only cultures that have been furthered or retarded by circumstances and whose advancement should be facilitated without being corrupted. Black should not copy white on the ground that it is suited to him.

His business is to foster "black power" by moving in the direction of human progress, making use of the common knowledge explosion as well as of ecumenical religious research.

We should avoid also the racism that sees only the advanced state of our culture and the backwardnesses of others—as though our thinking had not had setbacks and losses in important domains which not all those we consider inferior have had. The Western technocracy that disregards love and the will is certainly not an example of progress. In this respect the cultures associated with Yoga and Zen are in the lead.

Modern dialogue is not simply between individuals but, through the medium of individuals, among human groups. What is needed is to promote the complete economic development of the groups that lagged behind at the time of the sudden scientific and economic advance of the West, which had the "know-how" to exploit to its profit the riches of the world. This development cannot be induced from the outside by opposing local ways and imposing on a whole country the Western way of life. Local initiatives must be helped. The poor are not minors to be protected and provided with whatever they lack. Like the preceptor of the adolescent, the technical adviser must be trained for authentic human relations based upon dialogue and exchange.

To love one's neighbor as oneself is not to want to make him identical with oneself. A country where all the men were poured out of the same mould would be a hell. Life situations must be equalized by struggling against the injustices that do not permit everyone to realize his potentialities: but the objective must not be to impose uniformity.

Racist apartheid is an error, above all because it aims to preserve the wealth of the race that thinks itself superior; yet the universal crossbreeding of individuals and cultures would not be a happy solution. Man finds his equilibrium in belonging to a human group having its own traditions; he suffers when he is *déraciné*. Cosmopolitanism is not an ideal. A man is an authentic citizen of the world only insofar as he is first of all a conscientious citizen who loves his own small country. Today when man is less and less in a position to take his destiny into his own hands, he should reflect upon what would be best for him. It is best to preserve the human riches embedded in the mosaic of civilizations and cultures by means of dialogue between them, in a collaboration having the progress of humanity as its end. Perhaps it is not yet too late to do this at this juncture when Marxism is questioning itself about the possibility of different approaches to socialism, at the moment when the post-Vatican Council Church is recognizing that Catholic truth may be expressed in different cultures—and not perforce in the Latin language.

CHAPTER 7

VALUING OR DEVALUING LOVE

IN ITS CURRENT MEANING the word *love* is inseparable from sexuality. It stands for that mysterious affinity that urges two beings of different sexes to unite more completely in the satisfaction of their genital need. So intensely sexualized has the word become that one is reluctant to use it to express the norm of human existence or the religious relation. Nevertheless it is legitimate to speak of love for a good wine, love of self, love of one's neighbor, love of God.

Having thus generalized on love, we may state that sexual

love is only one particular instance of it. And it is important to bring sexual love back into the general framework of love, for the reason that, contrary to the prevailing outlook, the voluptuous satisfaction of desire in physical harmony is not everything. For a love to succeed physically between a man and a woman there must first of all be a worthwhile relation between two human persons—and this too is the exception. To love one's neighbor as oneself applies also to one's marriage partner, and is essential to the success of the marriage. Unfortunately it is necessary to emphasize this obvious fact. For the most charitable people, the ones most deeply involved and most open to dialogue are often totally lacking in charity and most unsuited to conjugal and family dialogue when they come to settle down and relax in their own homes.

And this is not surprising. In fact, contrary to what might seem to be the evidence, the relation between the man and woman who love each other is particularly difficult, for sexuality places an obstacle in its way. But how does this sexual aspect, which serves the specific love of man and woman, hinder that love?—Simply because sex can utterly complicate the human social relation.

Sex appears to be the enemy of love, whereas it actually should raise its value, but this is simply because we love with or in spite of our sex, since we do not know how to use our sex in order to love, and we do not love our sex. Love vanishes in the automatisms of desire, or else it endeavors to deny the existence of sex by divesting itself of flesh and blood. Hence we must lay stress upon the impossibility of sexless love. Love must have a sex since we have a sex. How should we use it correctly? Very simply, by understanding the significance of sex, which is devalued when it is reduced to genital satisfaction.

In our erotic civilization, love is king. Yet this love has become anti-love, a social scourge. And why?—Let us, if we dare, take a good look at it. What we see is males and females in search of their prey; the tragedies of prostitution, of pornography, of adultery, of sexuality among youngsters, of divorce, of contraception or excessive births. And so far we have mentioned only what is known as normal sex. Is this *love*, this ungovernable drive of the human animal that has been named instinct?—erroneously, we add, since animal instinct is an instrument of order and discipline.

Sex is opposed to an interpersonal relation. Either we let it take its course and the other person is nothing more than a thing, a prey, an object of egotistical pleasure satisfying a need, at best an accomplice in sexuality; or else we do our utmost to cut out sex. In that case we become repressed, we endeavor to avoid encounters with the dangerous opposite sex, we inhibit our emotional life or our sociability in order to avoid shocks, and so we become neurotics of isolation.

Contrary to appearances, the relation between a man and a woman is the most difficult one there is. For it joins two beings of different psychism and behavior who rarely succeed in understanding one another and are tempted either to despise or to envy one another in a racist way in which the man thinks that he is superior, and often is believed by the woman to be so (unless she is the one who assumes the superior role). And these two beings, for whom the relation is difficult, now find that as always when the difference is considerable it becomes even more considerable if desire carries all before it. They succumb to it with satisfaction or with shame, but they feel very keenly that this automatic and hurried act has an inhuman quality. Hence the dissatisfaction of the Don Juans and the libertines who sense very well that love is something quite different.

Yet we have the tendency to see this difficulty of dialogue between a man and a woman chiefly within the framework of the physical relations of the couple. We think often that sex is a domain apart which concerns us at certain times, but that there

is something else to life and that this something else has nothing at all sexual in it. If we were told that all our social
relations are concerned with sex, in other words that they are
sexual relations, carnal relations, we should be shocked. And
yet, how could it be otherwise? We are not neuter beings in
relations with other neuter beings; we are not pure spirits. We
are beings of flesh and blood, men or women in relations with
men or women. How can this be eliminated from the relations,
how can we forget sex and the flesh? Nevertheless this is what
we habitually try to do, and that is why we succumb when sex
and the flesh, having been neglected, take their revenge.

Every social relation is sexual because it is a relation between
two sexed beings and because the primordial interest of the
interhuman relation is not simply in dialogue and the collaboration of aptitudes and cultures, but also under the complementary conditions of the masculine and the feminine.

This is precisely what is contested by the modern spirit,
based as it is on the cultural plasticity of the masculine and of
the feminine, for it would assert that there is neither masculine
nor feminine—at least on the psychological and sociological
plane, since all orientations are possible. Man and woman are
equal, they are two varieties of humanity: we must be fully
convinced of this scientific observation. The woman is not a
small complement of the masculine norm. She is a true fraction
of the human species, complementary in equality, each fraction
being incomplete without the collaboration of the other. God
created them man and woman, which is not to say that the
norm is the couple, but that the human being requires the
collaboration of the masculine and of the feminine, as much in
social as in family life.

Why do we so often reject the fact of the equality of man and
woman? Because we think that to be equal means to be identical. Now in this case the equality lies in the total difference. A
certain variety of feminist sees Utopia in the claim of being

identical, not complementary. To be sure, this does not mean refusing to recognize anatomy and physiology, but it does say that, apart from this "small" matter, man and woman are neuter beings for whom sexual difference does not exist.

This is a monstrous mistake, one that has a disruptive effect upon our whole society. Female frustration does not arise from the inadequacy of woman's nature, but from the fact that to be neuter is for a woman even more impossible than for a man, and that her effort to be neuter consists in trying to adapt herself to a society conceived by men for functioning in as men. This is contrary to her nature, since she is not in fact a man. (There is a language problem here in giving the same name to the species and to its masculine variety. To speak of masculine man seems a pleonasm, and one hardly dare speak of a feminine man!)

It is not a question of one's observing the rules of genuine virility in one's conduct, for, in pursuance of this, man perverts the aggressive and sensual sides of his nature and compels woman to pervert hers through coquetry and submission. To examine one's views upon female nature requires that one should understand masculine nature, which is also completely unknown. Men must be willing to reflect upon the problems of their nature and not feel satisfied with their habit of dissociating reason from feeling, thus splitting their lives into two parts, one being apparently neuter and the other sexual.

A man is a being all of whose cells have the chromosome Y which is responsible for virility, and whose testicles constantly secrete the male hormone which influences through the blood stream all the organs and notably the brain. A woman complementarily is a being all of whose cells have a second chromosome X instead of Y and whose ovary is at the origin of a diphasic hormonal cycle subjecting the whole system and the brain to the double crisis of the menstrual period and that of ovulation. The famous "pill," known as the contraceptive pill, is in reality a hormonal derivative holding up ovulation. Its obvious harm lies in that it affects the woman's natural processes by suppressing her cycle, as I have elaborated in my books *La dignité sexuelle* and *Amour et contraception* (both 1965).

Genetic and hormonal differences are at the source of the masculine and feminine views of the physical and the moral. Both masculine and feminine outlooks can be shaped entirely by culture, but the question is to decide what is legitimate and what is not. And what is more, whatever customs and situations dictate, the woman cannot forget that she is a woman and the man a man. The ideal society is not one in which an effort is made to make man and woman uniform by means of a false identification—which is contrary to the nature of both—but one in which they are able to expand in complementary collaboration. A human action is complete only through masculine and feminine participation, whether it be a family or a professional project.

But we are mistaken not only in thinking of ourselves apart from our genital organs, as neuters, in forgetting our chromosomes and our hormones, which sexualize our whole being. We also labor under the conviction that we have an ungovernable sexual need we believe to be an instinct, something that is altogether self-evident in the man and would be so too in the woman if custom were to permit to her what many women desire. Would it not be right, in the name of equality, to set woman free by making her as much a slave to her sensuality as the man traditionally is, to replace the "duty" of behaving with foolish ignorance by the "duty" of indulging in a hygienic mating and loveless orgasmo-therapy? This would be just as absurd and as much to be pitied.

In fact we have seen that human sexuality does not flow from conflict between instinct and morality. Man instinctualizes his desire when he follows customs that are mere prejudices, and forgets that it is *human* sexuality only when the union is humanized by cerebral control of his sensuality—that is, when it is subjected to reason.

The brain is actually the organ of self-control, although without intending to we have made it the organ of sensuality or of neurosis (through repression). This is self-control not for its own sake, but at the service of the superior values of love, or what in the language of morality is called chastity.

Continence and chastity are considerably downgraded today, and even made to sound ridiculous. To a certain extent this can be laid at the door of a negative morality that has allowed us to think that what was involved was a kind of castration in which the genital organs were simply not used. This is why people often think that chastity requires ignorance—if not indeed horror—of sex, that it consists in the absence of desire or temptation, that it demands that the flesh be ignored in behalf of the spirit and that one's feeling and all attraction toward another person be repressed. Chastity of this kind is a most fertile source of neurosis, but it is not human chastity. It is the enemy of sex, whereas true and positive chastity allows the full appreciation of the values of sex only when placed at the service of love.

Chastity is not a question of not having sexual relations or "bad" thoughts but a question of the spirit in which one regards the functions of sex—and this obtains whether one is a totally continent celibate or a married person, that is, one who normally has sexual relations.

Chastity rests upon the spirit of clear-sightedness that enables us to know how to love (we have already defined its psychophysiological methods). Chastity means being free in the face of our sexual need so that we will not be driven by this need to do appalling things. This need could normally be satisfied only within the framework of an interpersonal relation that allows for its necessity—that is, in the case of a man and a woman who have recognized the need to form a couple, the complete and final community of life. This is the conjugal love of which the genital aspect is only one necessary consequence.

Genital satisfaction is perforce and by nature abnormal when it is outside that meaning, whether it involves a solitary egotistical satisfaction that is not a relation, or a perverted relation, or a "normal" relation carried on between two partners without real love. In the human species it is not two organs, two erotisms, that are united. It is two persons body and soul who are united; and this is possible only within the framework of a positive communion. Contrary to various preconceptions, real love is of necessity unique.

It does not follow that the celibate and the couple are, as people think, in an opposite sexual situation. For both, continence is necessary. For the celibate it is not only a matter of doing nothing. It is a matter of knowing oneself to be fully a man or fully a woman having social relations with men and women. Chastity alone makes this possible by triumphing over the temptation to limit one's concept of sex to sexual desire and sentimentality. The person who is not chaste alternates between desire and neutrality; the person who is chaste, who has learned to be chaste, normally has desires and temptations but he contends against them. He can see the other sex, not as a prey nor as a neuter comrade, but in its complementary riches, which are to be observed in all the conditions of life where the woman and the man have need of their reciprocal judgment, something impossible where they are either neuter or uncontrolled.

Paradoxically then, as we see, it is to the extent that we struggle against the vested exploitation of erotism that we shall raise the value of sex again in the estimation of the individual and of society, contrary to the attitude of the two enemies of sex—the libertines and the puritans, both of whom are strangers to its real value.

But chastity and continence are necessary also to the sexual expansion of conjugal love. This is incomprehensible to anyone who identifies continence with the absence of sexual relations. The married couple are not brother and sister, and they do not have to live as brother and sister. But this is the relation generally offered to them with the aim of spacing or limiting births, whether for a prolonged period with the result certain, or for interrupted periods based on current knowledge of the woman's fertility, with the result less certain.

When this type of continence (i.e., lacking the spirit of chastity), which seems to be the only genuine contraceptive process designed to limit births, is propounded to people who are without self-control and thus not equipped to practice it, they become imbalanced through separation and the suppression of unsatisfied desire.

Since it is often a duty to limit fertility for demographic or family reasons, and since it would be failing in love to have limitless fertility (often the sign of masculine egoism), people have come to look upon as normal the contraceptive processes not requiring continence. This is because the harmfulness of such processes has not been understood: processes that pervert the nature of the sex act or the female cycle, and as the result of their failures lead to the horrors of therapeutic or clandestine abortion—the prenatal assassination that is not the less horrible when achieved earlier by means of drugs preventing development, or of appliances fixed in the uterus at the risk of irritating, infecting, or causing cancer. This is what is forced upon the woman as a method of prevention by the ignorant egoism of the man and of the technocrat. The nature of the man or the woman may also be seriously modified by that final mutilation known as surgical sterilization.

Why do we have these horrors, so damaging to love, while sexuality appears to be the enemy that must at all costs be satisfied? The answer is that it is not understood that the spirit of chastity and relative continence, which controls sensuality and desire vis-à-vis love, is necessary to the sexual growth of the couple. That being so, it would seem that if adults cannot control themselves they must be recognized as still adolescents and their healthy matings legalized short of marriage, since they are not yet qualified for marriage.

On the same premise, the celibate must be seen as the unfulfilled misfit who is incapable of development in his abnormal situation and for whom marriage offers the only hope of retrieving his balance. And indeed marriage could have just such a happy outcome, but only where it was a forced continence that had turned the celibate into a neurotic via repression and isolation. What will restore his balance then will not be the sexual relation but *affection*. One will grant, of course, the possibility of an exceptional penitential ascetic celibacy where imbalance is accepted in view of a higher good, but it is understood that such a concept is not favorable to a balanced, consecrated celibacy. It results in squarely opposing the priest to the married couple, and in asserting his total incompetence in conjugal affairs, whereas chastity concerning love has a very different approach to the duty of the priest, as likewise to that of the married couple.

How resolve this problem?—Only by acknowledging our mistakes in what concerns human sexuality as obstacle to love. While from the viewpoint of elementary biology, sexual differentiation is geared to fertility at the service of the continuity of the species, it has created other functions in the human species. Generally the object of union is set over against the object of procreation. But it is chiefly regarded as sensual assuagement. In reality the primary role of sexuality is to differentiate the human race into complementary variants, in an individual and social teleology that does not concern the genital organs other than as producers of hormones, and hence a teleology that is essentially *continent*.

The second human role of sexuality is not to generate general simple attraction between men and women, but to engender the selective attraction that makes a man and a woman a *couple* founded on a special dimension of love. Here again, whatever is commonly thought, the genital activity is secondary. One does not love, one does not marry another person to satisfy a desire; one desires the other person because one loves him or her and wishes to be more closely united. A couple who build their marriage on desire or eroticism or sentimentality are building on very weak foundations. Preparation for marriage requires a clear intelligence for the appreciation of genuine love; for genuine love is one not blinded by eroticism or sentimental feelings.

Two people marry because they have a *reflective* intuition that they will be able to live their whole lives together. The durability of marriage requires that the union be not merely sensual (without which, however, love would run the risk of diminishing and disappearing). True love means understanding and dialogue between the couple in a *community of life*. Here again, chastity is indispensable. Periodic continence is a divisive factor in a couple who do not know how to love, but an expanding factor for love to those who know how to profit from it so as to love better even without genital union. And when old age comes along, the diminution of genital activity diminishes nothing of the love. Conjugal love is not an alternation of spirit and flesh; it is always love at once spiritual, emotional, and physical, even in total continence, for it is based on education of the cerebral control that frees us from ungovernable desire.

But when we consider the twofold finality of the genital act itself, the relative continence of the cerebral control also plays an essential role in it. Most frequently union takes place through desire. But what is desired? Not primarily to assuage a need or to seek enjoyment. Today our mis-education in sexuality makes pleasure the prime objective, emphasizing the immense yield of pleasure partaken of in the difficult harmonizing of two rhythms—difficult simply because the man, having insufficient control as a result of his bad habits, is not successful in rousing the woman.

The aim of the union is not pleasure, which is only an accompaniment and must be controlled to avoid falling into the unconsciousness of a fleeting automatism. It is the communion of two personages, body and soul, flesh and spirit, *in the course* of the sex act, and it demands the quasi-mystical consciousness of the joy of being united. The ineffable *joy* that climaxes the human interpersonal relation will never be known by those who do not know how to use their normal cerebral power of control. No one who has acquired this power (which is the norm) need fear coming too rapidly to a climax; he is not obliged to scamp or suppress the preliminary caresses for fear of untimely and ungovernable release. This cerebral control places a man at the top of his human sexuality. It is not a genital automatism as in the case of the butterfly, to whose level the patron of striptease or prostitution debases himself, nor an automatic mating following the pattern of birds and mammals, but a permanent choice both loving and clear-sighted during every moment of the act, which is the true loving communion. That is what is meant by "to love as oneself" in the course of the sex act.

Finally we come to the aim of procreation. The couple do not marry for an egotistical love; they wish to found a family. But how achieve this? Is the child to be merely the product, undesired, of a mating automatism? Couples who have been drawn together more by spiritual considerations take offense at being told that the principal end of their union is the child, for it seems to suggest a strictly animal purpose to procreation. Human procreation requires not the blind release but the *cerebral control* of sensuality. This is what makes *voluntary procreation* possible. But genuine will is involved here, for volun-

tary procreation amounts to more than a decision not to oppose
conception any longer by the use of appliances or drugs.

Voluntary procreation is the decision of the couple in control
of their sexuality who choose what to do in regard to what they
legitimately desire: fertilization or not fertilization. Scientific
knowledge of the time of ovulation, notably by the temperature
rise and associated symptoms, allows of choosing (if they desire
a child) the physiological moment. Added to this is the control
by both parties of the unfolding of the sex act, so that they are
not compelled to have reached the level of fecund ejaculation if
this is not desired or if it would be desirable to avoid fecundation. Thus fecundation is fully willed and at the same time it is
possible to limit births without completely renouncing union.
Reflex control and knowledge of the sterile periods allow this
without difficulty for a couple who are disciplined and not
slaves of an ungovernable drive forcing them to separate from
each other to avoid catastrophes. There are cases where the
uncertain periods are long. This could be a catastrophe for the
couple not thus educated but not for the disciplined couple who
know how to indicate their tenderness with variations of union,
more or less intense, and for whom total continence within a
loving, conjugal, undivided context is not only possible but
actually enhances the value of love.

This is not a utopia reserved for élite couples who do not
experience intense sensuality. It is the norm of a genuine,
human, fully matured sensuality, respectful of the human dignity of sex, both one's own and that of the other person. Everyone can attain to it. If we have ever experienced the horrors we
are led into by an egoism that deprives us of the fullness of joy
for the fleeting enjoyment of a little sensuality, we have reason
enough to learn it, reason enough to believe in it.

While it is never too late, learning actually commences at
birth; and the secret of later sexual balance is to be found in
the sexual and emotional balance acquired before the age of

five in the unconscious imitation of the parental model. It is during this early stage that sexual neuroses have their origin, and we must take into account the valuable findings of psychoanalysis in this area, while having the good sense not to be confused by its inaccurate terminology for adult sexuality. What is in question here is anatomo-sociological sexuality and the ripening of emotion.

Sexual control will ultimately depend upon education in general control during childhood before puberty and on reassuring sex instruction that does not stop at anatomy and genital physiology but goes on to specify the *human* quality of sex.

But the adolescent period is especially crucial in avoiding the correlative errors either of those who advise early release from control, and so represent the use of sex as a purely physiological act of no importance, or of the legalistic moralists who think it enough to forbid pre-marital sex within the context of a negative, disembodied asceticism. It is the early sexual practices that cause the conviction that an uncontrollable sexual instinct blocks affectivity by a sensual, narcissitic egoism and thus prevents one from opening up to another.

The continence that should be held out to the adolescent is a positive kind, and from it flows a clear-sightedness that frees him to assess the true significance of sexuality instead of being enslaved by a mere drive. This is continence to the end of being better sexed and of growing up, of being capable of authentic relations with the other sex, of emotional maturation, of being able to love under the sexual aspect as well as all other.

Instead of developing his scruples by giving him a terror of masturbation, instead of letting things drift while waiting for this sign of immaturity to go of its own accord, the struggle against the temptation should be suggested as the means of learning self-control without losing heart over accidental falls. This should be achieved by the application of general self-control to a sexuality that has been thoroughly understood. Prayer and the sacraments should be resorted to not as aids in a struggle for ascetic holiness against a wicked nature but as a means, in the struggle against temptations to pervert nature, of becoming more completely natural, normal, and human by virtue of the supernatural not cut off from nature but giving it its full meaning.

But why should continence be proffered as the right thing?— Because continence will enable the adolescent to choose with clarity his or her true vocation, which is not marriage at any price in order to satisfy some desire. One's true vocation lies in deciding whether one is made for marriage or for celibacy, while recognizing that unsought celibacy (if one has not found a kindred spirit) is not a fatal catastrophe. Celibacy does indeed mean renunciation of marriage, of loving communion and of family, but it also means the retention of liberty for a more complete commitment. Viewed from this standpoint, marriage also should be seen as a renunciation: one is no longer an individual free to offer one's total commitment at will; one is only half of a couple responsible for the education of a family. Freedom therefore is at the option of the individual, and his choice should be inspired by clarity of vision and not by fear of either celibacy or marriage.

But a successful marriage is a difficult undertaking. The fact that there are so many failures is precisely because during adolescence relations between the sexes are seriously defective. They are cheapened by the sensual, erotic or sentimental approach, by the non-dialogue known as flirtation, which pairs off youngsters under the illusion of love. Or else, in order to avoid this, the two sexes are so rigorously segregated that they do not get to know each other at all but readily enough find the means to meet clandestinely for sensual association.

Future sexual balance on the individual, social, and conjugal planes requires this difficult apprenticeship in the right relation between male and female and mutual dialogue. There is no substitute for it. But in the name of this very knowledge (which is obstructed by puritan barriers), the great danger of libertinism must also be reckoned with. The current practice of premarital sex manages more than anything to preclude genuine love, for the transition has to be made from love to the genital and not the other way around. So it is positive chastity alone that enables one to know the other sex as such and to discover the genuine love that qualifies a pair to become engaged.—For the later serenity of the couple requires an engagement period entered into with a sense of responsibility. During this period loving one another will be examined as a way of life for two; it is not a period of sensual "billing and cooing" in a state of artificial euphoria from which they will awaken in despair.

To embark on genital relations before the legalization of marriage is, for one thing, to show oneself incapable of control, which is a danger signal for the future, and for another thing, to reveal anarchical tendencies by taking no account of society. Genital relations are the prerogative of a couple, and people do not become a couple simply through mutual engagement, but through solemn entry into the state of a couple in the civil community and the religious community. Physical union comes after that.

Marriage is a grave commitment, one that is of its nature final and indissoluble. Divorce is not something we are forbidden to seek, or even something we forbid ourselves. Divorce is unthinkable for those who have understood love, and it should never be considered as a future way out that justifies getting involved without thought. The solution is never divorce. The thing is to marry only after reflection, and thereafter to strive together to avoid misunderstandings while making love grow. For this love, however strong it may be, is only a seed to be cultivated and—it is important to realize—a very fragile seed. If really interested counselors could help separated couples, divorce might be avoided altogether. And when there are children, there is no choice between disagreement and separation: they are equally criminal. People have a duty to pull together if they are to be worthy of their human status. It is so easy to accuse the other person while refusing to look at one's own deficiencies. Faults are always on both sides.

But if one wants to love one's partner properly, there is a final apprenticeship to be served: the honeymoon. If during this time the newlyweds sink into the sensual and the sentimental, the marriage is in jeopardy even though the trouble may manifest itself only later in the form of an excessive fecundity that might seem to demand contraception. It is during the honeymoon that the couple should learn together to control the sensual reflexes, just as at periods of non-separated continence. This is not for the purpose of envisaging a later natural spacing of births, but in order to attain the joy of being together without continual desire, the joy of physical union of a calm and conscious kind; then eventually they may have their children as they wish.

We have seen how we can become unbalanced through the illusion of the spontaneity of love. We must learn to use fully the wonderful richness of sex. We shall then have true human spontaneity, like that of the athlete whose expertise we all admire but has in fact cost him no end of hard work. But when it comes to sex education we must not be left on our own. Beyond those (indispensable) specialists one should be able to count on, particularly in difficult cases, it is up to parents to help parents, up to couples to help engaged and other couples in the communal apostolate that discharges the duty of love in our social involvement. Schools for parents, counseling for the young, premarital instruction, marriage counseling, and other constructive programs are already mobilized or at least projected in many areas to counteract the poor remedy of artificial contraception and to restore the value of love to sexuality.

CHAPTER 8

LOVING THIS WORLD AND
MAKING IT LOVABLE

WE OUGHT TO LOVE one another: for this is what we were made for.—That is the end-message of psychobiological self-knowledge, and the message is confirmed by this self-knowledge, which specifies for us the technique of loving, the technique of being human, personalizing, *amorizing*. Being men as we are, we must love all men, each man for himself in his freedom to be himself and to be different. And we must love all the different groups to which men belong, and work not for their uniform identity but toward a dialogue that will respect their unique qualities.

But an assertion of universal loving solidarity such as this does not suffice to convince us of the role played by love in the world. An essential dimension is still missing—namely, what is the point of it all? Where is it leading? Is it enough to progress in the struggle for more balance and more happiness, and to help others to progress in the same way, generation succeeding generation in a perpetual beginning? Is the future to hold nothing better than this process repeated? Have the changes any meaning, are they leading to any progress? Are we on this earth only to perfect ourselves by means of altruistic individual effort?

The answer is not up to the religions, of whom the question should first be asked; it lies rather with science, which can even further increase the value of love for us.

In this immense universe, so terrifying and hostile, we have discovered an amazing secret, and its essence is that only a love-energy can account for the complexification afforded by its organizing forces. What counts is not the absurd, the incoherent, the horrible, which leap all too readily to the eye; on the contrary, what counts is that a meaning does exist. The world is evolving—in other words, it is under construction during the course of time, it is *progressing*. Nature may be likened to a work in which, whatever its causes and mechanisms, we can discern an ascent of love from the inanimate to the unicellular, from the unicellular to man. Consequently such a universe cannot be looked upon with cold detachment, for it has done everything in the face of a thousand contingencies (and perhaps innumerable other casualties), in order to progress as far as *us*—and we are perhaps not the only loving beings in the cosmos!

Made for love, we have been made by a work of love. We can

therefore cherish this universe, lovable in spite of everything, whence we have emerged. We need no longer feel that we are in it by virtue of some strange, extraneous accident. Despite our smallness, our role is essential since it is the deliberate outcome of an ascent of love, to the point where love becomes a thinking person and community of persons.

This *amorizing* universe has a message for anyone who, like Teilhard, consents to look at it with clarity of vision. Nature's task has not resulted in completed achievement; it has produced a being capable of this completion. The universe of tools and human techniques has succeeded to the universe of organo-implements shaped by the biological evolution of life, the creator of forms.

It is now up to humanity to pursue *the building up of the world,* not by using human intelligence to harness to its service a hostile universe in a state of Promethean revolt but by whole-heartedly devoting itself to other means.

The conservative mind regrets bygones and refers us to the lost paradise of primitive nature, forgetting that because man was disarmed and vulnerable, his nature was in a certain sense perverted in those times, since he was incapable of developing his aptitudes. The modern mind speaks to us enthusiastically of building up a new man better made for the exploration of the cosmos and for the concrete universe of the modern cities, forgetting in its turn an essential aspect—namely, that this kind of progress makes life intolerable for us, causes us to die of nervous fatigue and the diseases of civilization, dehumanizes us by cutting us off from nature, by making us into crowds of isolated individuals, the slaves of the technocrats.

What conclusion do we draw from all this? As always, that both are partly right: the conservative in his condemnation of the mistakes of so-called progress; the architect of this progress by his rejection of primitive nature and his abandonment to technology. Synthesis lies in rejecting an unthinking technology, in placing at the service of mankind a technology based on the satisfaction of true human needs, and in particular, a technology economically and politically relevant to man. (See on this point J. M. Paupert, *Pour une politique évangélique*.)

The conservative who wants to take us back to a nature that must be protected is right, but he is mistaken in thinking that this nature is pre-human, whereas actually it is human nature and it must be progressively unfolded and fulfilled by preserving its natural conditions, and in particular the nucleic acids, for which an increase of radioactivity would be fatal. It is the technologist's task then to realize the conservative's dream, to protect man in the wise up-building, through keeping to the blueprint of what man is called upon to be as the result of the potentialities inherent in him.

Man can do anything. With the pride of an adolescent technologist he wants to change everything no matter how—to modify his genes, the conditions of his development, his hormones, his sexuality, his brain, his psychism, his social relations; and to an increasing degree he has the power to do so. In a struggle against nature he is extending his mastery over the mechanisms of his thought and life. So long as he wisely limits himself to curing disease all is well. But as the result of industrialization and urbanization he is involuntarily forcing us into living conditions that are inimical to health. Then he sets about trying to ameliorate the lot of normal man, primarily by offering him anodynes to help him to sustain the difficulties of a life for which, in his capacity as technological man, he is partially responsible.

It is the task of science, which gives us such means, to implement morality by helping us to understand the meaning of the human phenomenon. Man is the outcome of an evolutionary ascent toward the finest human brain, allowing increased liberty, consciousness, and love. After the appearance of thinking man, evolution continued on another plane through cultural

progress, continuing in the same direction toward more consciousness and more liberty. Modern man has liberty in the
absurd power either to denaturalize that evolution by destroying himself or, on the other hand, to exploit it by hewing to the
natural processes and making better and better use of the
resources of the human brain. Thus we can follow the way
either of an irresponsible technocracy or of the beneficent exploitation of science and technology. Following this second way
will lead to new discoveries and the expansion of our natural
potentialities and phenomena.

What is the full meaning, then, of that duty of love that
shapes us? The duty is to love the world and the work being
completed in the world; it is to accept the interdependence of
everything surviving in the ascent of complexification which is
the Way of the Cross of life; it is to persevere in the struggle for
a more authentic and complete development. Time and the
future then take on their full meaning. We are not successive
generations hurled by chance into an absurd world where our
struggle has no value except for ourselves and for our contemporaries. Interdependence extends beyond the present. If we
have come this far it is because of the labors of those who went
before us. Our labor is the preparation of tomorrows, and we
must do our utmost to make tomorrows that will sing. We have
no right to betray our ancestors, and we have no right to betray
our heirs by handing over to them a world dissipated and
destroyed. Universal love is thus extended not only across space
but across time *to all humanity*.

The love of humanity is practiced first of all, as we have seen,
in the course of loving all men, for humanity has no existence
outside them. A totalitarian society can oppress men, a liberal
society can leave them to their misery; the human person will
never disappear in favor of a kind of social body in which it
would dissolve like the cells in our system. But the conditions of
man's expansion are contingent upon the nature of the society,

of the social structures, of the politics determining the framework of his life. And thus it is not enough just to love men; it is
necessary to participate with them in a collective humanistic
task. Development of a social framework more suited to the
personalizing of men in personalizing relations must be cease-
lessly promoted. Technological competence is indispensable for
such development, but it is not enough; it must be ordered
toward the common good. And the common good is the individual and social well-being that we call *amorization* and whose
conditions we must define more and more clearly.

At first we were concerned to remind the egotistical individual of today of his social dimension, of his need for others. But
this is not enough. Socialization is a great deal more than social
relations among men, it is the human task, the construction,
faithful to the dialectic of nature and to the vocation of man, of
a humanized world.

It is not enough to humanize social relations. The social
structures too must be humanized for they are the framework of
life, and they are also in a certain sense the organs of Teilhard's
noosphere, his personalistic society of human development.
(Nothing, e.g., is more certain to throw people off balance
than the gulf between private and public morality that deludes
people that they can be personally virtuous without exerting
themselves to improve society. People manage to be generous
and yet stand by while the social and economic structures fail
in generosity.)

Indeed, as Teilhard says, it is necessary to build a "common
front of human advancement." Was it not this common front
that Pope John XXIII labored to create by defining the conditions of a beneficent socialization, or by laying down, in *Pacem
in terris,* the rights and duties of citizens and of society, the
relations of individuals with one another in social life, the
relations between citizens and public authorities at the heart of
each political community, the relations among the different

political communities and the world community? It is this labor of humanist sociology, economy, and politics that today embodies the precept of loving one's neighbor as oneself. It is a question of seeing that man may not be crushed and destroyed by the fruit of his own activity.

Today people are developing a *forward look* beamed at building the future. This technological perspective on the future can operate only in the form of a choice, of what we prefer; to be complete this forward gaze must be a humanistic prospect interested in sacrificing neither the men of tomorrow nor the men of today.

We are in a world where automation, easing man's physical efforts—and even mental efforts insofar as they involve the mechanical—is going to leave us more and more free time to fill with leisure activities. Will man no longer know what to do with himself? How can we voice anxiety about leisure when we can barely make time for research, and everything has still to be done? Not only must we achieve self-conquest and help for others; the whole mobilization of the world for the service of man awaits our efforts. Those who have striven to achieve clarity of vision will realize that true charity means devoting oneself to creative collaboration. But this creation consists in more than merely remedying inadequacies. It is primarily concerned with the struggle to counter those terrible deviations caused by man's greatest sin—namely, the unthinking folly driving him to exploit his fellow man; to accumulate superfluous goods to satisfy his ego; and to accept the slavery of those social structures from which he profits at the expense of others. (We are quite as imbalanced when power is imposed on us by our social situation as when we choose it personally. This is the problem of amoral class morality.)

Understanding the meaning of love leads to restoration of love to its true place as a mover, like evolution, of history. Hence it is only in a confederation of communities developing on the human scale that man will find his own development. But, asks Teilhard, "Within that grandiose machine-in-motion which I visualise, what becomes of the pearl beyond price, our personal being? What remains of our freedom of choice and action?"

Freedom? "But do you not see," he replies, "that from the standpoint I have adopted it appears everywhere—and is everywhere heightened?"

"I know very well that by a kind of innate obsession we cannot rid ourselves of the idea that we become most masters of ourselves by being as isolated as possible. Yet is not the reverse the truth? We must not forget that in each of us, by our very nature, everything is in an elemental state, including our freedom of action. We can only achieve a wider degree of freedom by joining and associating with others in an appropriate way. This is, to be sure, a dangerous operation, since, whether it be a case of disorderly intermingling, or some simple form of co-ordination, like the meshing of gear-wheels, our activities tend to cancel one another out or to become mechanical—we find this only too often in practice.

"Yet it is also salutary, since the approach of spirit to spirit in a common vision or a shared passion undoubtedly enriches all; in the case of a team, for example, or of two lovers. Achieved with sympathy, union does not restrict but exalts the possibilities of our being. . . . A freedom, taken in isolation, is weak and uncertain, and may easily lose itself in mere groping. But a totality of freedom, freely operating, will always end by finding its road. . . . Only by reaching to the heart of the Noosphere . . . can we hope, and indeed be sure, of finding, all of us together and each of us separately, the fullness of our humanity."

But while Teilhard helps us to see what the task, our vocation of humanly organizing the earth and humanity, consists in, while he demonstrates the necessity for this task if the expansion of man is to be achieved, he does not fall into a utopian delusion that the task will be accomplished of itself, sweeping us along the while in a wonderful and inexorable way with the course of history.

The duty to devote ourselves to the salvation of humanity imposes upon us the duty to influence the course of history. Instead of submitting fatalistically to social, economic, and political determinisms, we have the duty to dominate them lest we perish. This is the same healthy morality essential to individual equilibrium, private relations between men, and public relations. Every human being, outside his examination of conscience on his own way of having, of being, and of acting vis-à-vis himself and others, should question himself about the behavior of all humanity in having, in being, and in acting.

Are we arrogantly going to want to conquer the whole cosmos in the guise of sorcerers' apprentices, or are we going to make up our minds to give priority to the humanization of the earth? Are we going to be destroyed in a technocratic activism, or are we seriously going to seek man's good (so vastly misunderstood)? Are we going to squander the riches of the world and pervert the nature of earth and man, or are we going to administer them and use them wisely? Are we going to set about studying the paramount problem of the moment—the better distribution of the goods of this world, the disappearance of hunger, of poverty, and of ignorance—or are we going to continue stupidly to expend for war the major part of the resources of humanity, the money of the poor? Will there never be a movement of public opinion sufficiently clear-sighted and courageous to force the heads of state to come out of their dreamworld and face up to the crimes for which they make themselves responsible by preferring the ways of violence, of power, and of pride, when there is only one valid human policy: that of the Sermon on the Mount?

It is through the power of gentleness and tenderness that the world will be built. But to bring that about, the leaders of this world must learn to love on the public plane of politics and economics as well as on that of their private relations. The art of governing by loving, not by particularism but in the real love respectful of others' liberty—would not this be the democratic ideal we are longing for?

CHAPTER 9

GOD IS LOVE

From the Science of Love to the Religion of Love

IN VIEW OF WHAT WE ARE, we have only a very vague idea of what we are. And so we have to supply the lack of the instinctive automatisms by the discovery of morality if we are going to conduct ourselves properly.

But it is not enough to conform to a moral code: we must also understand it. It must come naturally to us, which is not to say that it should seem easy but simply that it conforms with what we are and with what is suited to what we are. We have

146

just seen how, in order to understand fully what love consists in and why it is necessary, we can draw from a complete comparative psychobiology precious revelations of what man is and his situation in a world in a state of cosmogenesis. A scientific study of love such as this shows clearly that it is involved in a *common,* objective, constituent human *value* which no one can call into doubt and which should unite all men whether their morality is secular or religious.

But a complete study of our need for love should not stop at that point. For we must reflect upon the conclusions to be drawn from this morality if we are to understand its full significance. A secular morality will be satisfied with the natural, impersonal justification of love, and with constructing an attainable ideal of life and society. The most complete type is presented to us in the work of Julian Huxley or, for instance, the reflections of Roger Garaudy on Marxist morality.

We must bear in mind, however, that we did not have to wait for science to articulate the principle that we must love our neighbors as ourselves. The thinkers who have revealed universal love most completely belong to the Judeo-Christian tradition, which unfolds via the Bible testimony a historic development in knowledge of love.

We underestimate the Bible if we think of it merely as a compilation of ready-made truths (albeit containing some horrifying incidents), whereas it was a record made to give us testimony of the way in which chosen men understood better and better what God was revealing to them of himself and of their situation. And for Christians the Bible culminates in the historic Christian fact—namely, the incarnation of God in Jesus Christ. The Incarnation gave Revelation its supreme dimension and forged a new link between man and God by instituting the Church; for the Church is the sacred aspect of human society and its history, and within it the work of theologians helped by mystical experience and grace has cleared the way for study and greater understanding of the data of the origin of Revelation.

Because the law of love is already acknowledged to be the confirmation of Christianity, it would be only theoretically possible today to set out to discover this law *de novo* by means of a scientific study of man. One could at best attempt to verify one's knowledge without trying to fit the facts to it. For despite the objectivity of his approach, the researcher will always be in danger of being confused by the concordance between science and Christianity. Indeed, the harmony between the morality of science and Christian morality may be too perfect! Yet this should not be a matter for protest on the part of the Christian. For him such harmony should be obvious unless he has made the mistake of separating science and faith—as though one could isolate matter from spirit in the world and in man. Such scientific research therefore will have for the Christian a supplemental interest: it should not only recall to him this character common to all men, but also help him understand better that *faith in heaven is faith in the world.*

If there is thus a *convergence and harmony* between science and morality as the result of scientific progress, this should prompt the unbeliever to inquire into the truth of the Christian fact, which led its followers to understand love long before science did. True, this understanding has often been unfaithful to Revelation on account of Manichean and Jansenist temptations to transform the Christian realism of the earth into an idealism of heaven, historical communal salvation into an individual salvation through suffering.

There is no question here, of course, of trying to prove the existence of God-love in the name of the science of love which lays down the material conditions of love though quite incapable of telling us what this love is; for it is no less mysterious for having been objectively discovered.

In an absurd world where all is struggle, violence, and incoherence, the Christian message seems to have been parachuted into a reality that does not respond to it. On the contrary—and without denying the absurd, the incoherent, and the horrible—as soon as one perceives the guiding hand of the cosmogenesis of *amorization,* this world in laborious ascent of love (which necessarily includes failures) assumes a quite different aspect, even in the very significance of the failures. For failures may now be seen as no more than the inevitable setbacks of a natural work endowed with an *autocreative* power, a kind of nameless "pre-liberty" of matter in evolution; and one cannot help thinking how logical Christianity is, to speak to us of a God-love.

If the most clear-sighted of today's materialists are not led to religion by the altitude to which scientific materialism attains, it is because they are shutting themselves up in science and making no effort to infer its logical consequences from the outside. Science reveals to us the teleology of ascent, love, meaning in matter. Are we going to deny that this is a mystery that should open our eyes to another light? We hear that certain (more logical) people prefer to deny, in favor of fundamental absurdity, the meaning that science is discovering, but this of course is to set oneself against science itself.

The unaided powers of human reason are not sufficient to enlighten us fully as to why there is love in the world. True, philosophical research leads to what have been called the proofs or the natural or rational demonstrations of the existence of God; but however valid they may be, they do not convince us of the real existence of God. They are the arguments of probability in favor of a principle—i.e., the God of the philosophers and the scholars, a solely conceptual elaboration of what is suggested by a simple logical reflection on the world, whether starting from science or starting from common sense.

This common sense is conspicuously lacking in the intellectuals, yet it was found, for instance, in a certain Marseilles docker who, we are told, became filled with enthusiasm for the beauty of living matter as he saw it for the first time under Père Loew's microscope, and received the faith immediately. Why shouldn't the scientist be converted by the quite insufficient scientific explanation for the material conditions of this beauty? Why should the docker be converted? The Christian knows that the docker was the one with the grace of seeing, the grace that blinding intellectualism hinders people from receiving. This grace is a mystery, given to all but received by few—for there must be human participation. Lucidity and pliancy are called for, for precisely in this lies the secret of good-will that is expressed in psychophysiological terms as being relaxed, as not having, in the words of Père Carré, a stiff neck and a heart of stone!

Only by failing in objectivity could a scientist, looking at love, pass over the Christian message in silence. Christianity tells us that to love one's neighbor as oneself is the second commandment and that it cannot be separated from the first: to love the Lord our God. Our physical need of love should not then concern solely the world and men, it ought to be addressed to the Creator. But Christianity goes even farther. All love, it teaches, is a delegation of the love of God: we must love through Him, with Him, in Him: *per ipsum* et *cum ipso* et *in ipso;* all love is communal union of men in Christ.

Such a conception, which for the Christian is a reality, does not alter natural morality, but it gives it a quite different meaning and significance. The supernatural does not just add other obligations; rather, it makes us understand the whole significance of the love of men and of the love of the world within the framework of the love of God. We do not love God additionally, for God, in spite of His transcendence, cannot be dissociated from the world and from men, who exist only through the delegation of the powers of His permanent creative act. Natural morality is a morality of the immanence of love in the world. Christian morality links this immanence to a personal presence of a love existing in itself. Christianity, Rahner tells us, is a religion of the absolute future which is God. It is also a religion where the absolute future is *absolute love.*

It is Christianity that teaches us that God is love, that He loves us, that we can—therefore we must—love Him, and that the whole human task, individual and social, must be envisaged within a spiritual perspective. In this purview Christianity takes on the dimension of eternity, it reveals its worth as a collaboration in a divine work transcending space-time, it is the full meaning of space-time. And if Christianity so teaches us, it is as the fruit of its endeavor to understand what God has revealed of Himself by means of His prophets and His Son, Jesus Christ. But what has been revealed to us is not a message from beyond, from on high, concerning another world where we shall go later. Rather, it is the secret of this world here, and it allows us to understand better and to play more effectively our role on earth: to be in heaven instead of hell here and now.

One who believes—that is, the person who has faith, not purely sentimentally or purely intellectually but integrally (which means the passionate involvement of his whole being in a mystical relation with Another), and is nourished by this relation through prayer and the sacraments—this man may ask himself how he believes, may seek to discover how the need to love God is expressed and realized in him by the same mechanisms by which he is made lovable to God and is loved by God, and how he can love the world and men in God.

Once again there is no question of mixing science with faith. But the person who believes does not admit barriers: he believes with his whole being through the mechanisms of his being, and faith puts him in contact with its profound meaning. Mysticism is of necessity *neuromysticism.* To be sure, the unbeliever will be able to understand this neuromysticism or this sociomysticism only as a rational potentiality of the believer, and cannot be sure that it is genuine; yet even he will find in it a better way of communicating with his own ideal. For the believer this is none other than the immanence of God.

Before outlining the potentialities of a Christian neuromysticism and sociomysticism (which are *neurotheology* and *sociotheology*) we must briefly recall the Christian arguments proving that God is love because He loves the world and more especially because He loves men. Revelation regarding the love of God for the world has necessarily meant that something of the mystery of mysteries, which is the very being of God, has been made known to us. Human love is relational; so is divine love, expressed in the fact that God is love in relation because He is what we call the holy Trinity. However remote from us this revelation is, it is in agreement with the dynamism of love and appears logical to anyone who knows love. The logic, however, does not replace nor exhaust the mystery.

The role of sound apologetics here is not to replace faith by science or science by faith: it is to make the message of both science and faith better understood, together with demonstrating the fact that, far from opposing one another, they complement and call upon one another. Yet, however logical faith is, it remains faith—that is, confidence in Revelation, and therefore in a revealing God and in the Church, His interpreter.

Logical reflection leads us to a religion natural to man, and to a religious need more logically and completely satisfied by Catholic Christianity, which best expresses the religious aspirations of human nature. Yet like everything natural and human, this Christianity demands an awareness of the hidden meaning of things and beings, and an involvement not at all natural to the common appetite for what is easy. "A faith normally difficult," Père Roqueplo calls it: difficult like everything natural and human, yet more difficult even than that, in that it goes beyond what is natural and hence demands more confidence.

This is precisely Teilhard's testimony, for he did not hesitate to declare that if it fell to him to make the impossible choice between faith in the world and faith in God he would take the risk of faith in the world, since faith in the world, logically and fully understood, implies faith in God. Nevertheless he too recognized that despite the infallible logic that led him from the electron to the Omega point and the universal Christ, the cosmic Master of evolution, he was still amid "the shadows of faith." He who saw told us mysteriously that to believe is not to see. And his tremendous synthesized construct was for him what he already believed: a vision compelling him to involve himself even if it were not a matter of scientific certitude in the usual sense of the word.

Creative Love

What proof does Christianity give us that God is love, and that God loves us? Primarily there is the proof of *the creation*. God is not an indifferent architect who works out a calculation vis-à-vis the world. Creation is God's love poem for His smallest and most infinitesimal creatures as related for us by Genesis. God is certainly not the bearded old gentleman who shapes matter, and the materialists were right to replace this concept with the laws of matter. No, the God of Christians is a God of enthusiastic (even at times humorous) love. The élan of love that all but obliges God to create yet for all that does not constrain His liberty—that is what we mean by love. Although complete and sufficient in His eternal transcendence, which comprises everything that is, was, and will be, God nevertheless incorporates in His temporal immanence, emphasized by the Incarnation, all the fecundity of His love. And this fecundity is the source of Creation's progression from the simple, multiple, inexistent, and virtual toward unity. To create is to unite, Teilhard tells us, and to unite is to love, it is to will progress.

When today science catches a glimpse of love at the heart of the world, why shouldn't this turn us toward the Christian God? This is the whole Teilhardian apologetic of the Omega point drawing the world toward that Forward and Upward where there is convergence. A world that is personalized suggests a personal and personalizing Center that from the beginning is responsible for the personalization.

No one who is using his head would take the basis of atheistic materialism to be the properties of matter that science lays down—namely, that the greater emerges from the less, that everything derives from matter in evolution, that quantitative complexification is the source of new qualities. For the mystery of these properties of matter is very simply the mystery of the immanence of God. Hence, to see superiority and spiritual newness emerging from the organization is sufficient to suggest that the immanence has a relation with a transcendence without which it would be impossible for something greater to emerge from something less, or for quality to derive from quantity. In proving the impossible, science in fact nullifies materialism for us by producing as a religious argument the very arguments upon which atheism is based.

If such arguments have been used, and can still be used, in behalf of atheism it is because, whether we believe it or not, we Christians in general give a very poor accounting of God and His creative power. To believe in God seems to lessen the value of the world and of liberty. Now, modern man very rightly insists upon the values of the world, of man, and of liberty. What the modern world does not realize is that in rejecting God and admitting that the world is absurd it is devaluing the world, which is not absurd, and thereby providing technocracy with the temptation to reject every standard in the name of a false Existentialist liberty.

The modern world needs God, not as a remedy for ignorance and impotence but to give meaning to its magnificent striving for knowledge and technological advancement. *The value of the world and of human effort is the "sign of the times" that ought to lead us back to God.* To achieve this a right vision—the orthodox Christian vision of God and of Creation—is necessary. The technician does not create, he manufactures by modeling inert matter according to his own taste. Such an act is not a creative act. God alone creates by calling into being—that is, by organizing and individualizing matter, and by delegating His powers to the properties of such matter.

This is the example to imitate: because God is love He is not an oppressive tyrant; He leaves to His creature a certain autonomy that is more manifest as its organization is greater—that is, where God has endowed it with greater aptitudes. To say that matter evolves as the result of its own properties, and to say that God creates, is to state two aspects of the same thing: God creates in an *evolutionary creation* through the properties of matter. The apparent materialism of science lies in the fact that the laws of creation are being considered from their material angle, but this by no means excludes the complementary metaphysical angle, the spiritual aspect of the laws.

The Church rightly condemns pantheism and immanentism. These are the negation of God, whose essential reality is the transcendence that makes Him personal, that makes Him absolute love. These two erroneous doctrines are the equivalent of modern materialism and remain the great temptation of many modern minds that see the spirit only as an *emergence* from the properties of matter. But even when the Church condemns a doctrine as false, there is always a grain of truth in it. In such doctrines the portion of truth—and it is true—concerns the value of the world. This value was misunderstood by the Manichean or Gnostic deviations, which separated the world and God as completely as possible.

One must beware of a too great respect that dissolves God into the "beyond" where He becomes a useless magician, so exiled from nature that it then becomes totally autonomous. To respect God is to respect His work, it is literally *to make holy again* a profane world and not to sunder the profane from the sacred, for that would keep it profane while the sacred is excluded as a useless superstructure, whose importance contracts to the status of a sort of outer skin. The sacred is in fact the deep dimension of the profane. One must never, therefore, oppose pantheism without also opposing "transcendentalism." The *good pantheism* dear to Teilhard, defender of the values of the world, is the immanence of the transcendent God, the complete concept of God. In such a concept of the world the properties of matter and free human technical constructiveness are in no way opposed to God. Man the *co-creator* is called to the holy and sacred task of completing creation, with God acting through man's freedom, which must be faithful to the meaning inherent in things.

Redemptive Love

But the love of God is seen not only in this positive aspect of the value of the world and of the human task; it is, paradoxically, seen also in the negative aspect that hinders many from believing in a good God. The world is not perfect, for it is not God. Indeed, weren't there all manner of horrible contingencies, made worse by the processes of nature, even before the appearance of man, who only aggravated the trouble by his sin? Besides, is it good to have given such power to man, who is so stupid and inadequate? The secret of God's love lies precisely in this. There is no love if there is no liberty, and there is no liberty without stupidity, without disobedience, without the power to say No. There is no ascent without descent, no summit without an abyss.

One might reproach a God who is only a maker with His mistakes and failures: he is no longer God. With a God who is love, a God who delegates His powers and respects His creatures' autonomy, it is a different matter. God does not carry matter and man toward the heights. He gives them the power to ascend by struggling against whatever holds them back; but the power of ascending cannot be conceived except against the possibility of a fall. Without constant miraculous intervention by God (which would not be creation, for He would not be acting through love but through coercion), it is obviously unthinkable that, e.g., the nucleic acids may not develop into a virus or that man may not succumb to evil. That does hinder certain nucleic acids from supporting the evolution toward man; nor does it hinder saints from struggling against sin. As the general pattern of life indicates, the danger inherent in liberty gives value to the struggle. Paradoxically, the evil of the world adds to its value, for it enhances the good, which is now no longer an insignificant automatism but rather a triumph, a victory. God's victory is that material creation can produce a being capable of loving freely.

It is precisely the evil of the world that allows us to appreciate better the truth that God is love. The adventure of matter and its crowning distinction, man, has all the appearances of a Way of the Cross. The cross is the opacity of the natural order, of matter and of the flesh, that often dooms to failure what had been fashioned for success. A world thus made by love needs to be saved. This we know to be the Christian thesis. God was made man and became the Savior, the Redeemer of men through His death on the cross. Unfortunately the modern world, which more than ever needs this thesis of redemption because of the urgency and importance of its task, totally ignores it because no one has succeeded in making its importance understood.

That God might create Adam and Eve at the origin of humanity, two perfect beings, not intended for suffering and death, endowed with all knowledge including the vision of God; that they were driven from Paradise for having contravened a divine interdict and for having freely chosen to know good and evil; that their "fall" caused them to lapse into savagery, suffering, and death in separation from God; that to expiate this *original* sin, which seems to have stricken unjustly all the descendants of the first couple, the Incarnation had to take place whereby the suffering of the Just One compelled the pardon of God—the modern world sees in all this an uninteresting legend apparently at odds with scientific knowledge and involving an unjust God and an inscrutable avenger.

We trust that theological investigation carried out in the spirit of enlightenment and deepening research—which is the spirit of Vatican Council II—may succeed in presenting such biblical data more effectively without changing the essence of the dogmas, so that the modern world may live by them instead of laughing at them. What appears unintelligible to us is precisely what is essential to the understanding of man.

We must reconcile the Adam of science and the Adam of faith. The Adam of science is not a kind of animal; he is rather the first free and responsible man because he is a man and no longer an animal. His lack of culture does not matter; he is nonetheless fully man, with man's greatness, man's freedom, and man's weakness—the weakness of that freedom, which means that he is corporeal and tempted to fall below his potentialities. To emerge into freedom in the manner of the adolescent means to demand total autonomy, to succumb to the prideful desire to follow one's own inclination; it means that man, though capable of being humanized, becomes dehumanized and falls into ruin.

This is precisely what we are told by Genesis. And as a result of the fact that from the time of the first man and ever since, man has possessed this *weakness,* due to his corporeal constitution, of falling into evil, the world has been in a *state of fall.* Who could deny this when contemplating the modern world and what is happening to its wonderful potentialities? But let us not accuse Adam in order to excupate ourselves. He was only the first one who behaved stupidly, though capable of wisdom; we continue to do the same thing. We are all companions in evil. But Genesis has the wisdom not to identify the state of original sin with deliberate sin.

It may be objected that Adam, being uncivilized, was not ready for his responsibility; but this is to forget that he was nonetheless fully man—that is, he was no longer bound by his instincts; and he was asked to undertake the adventure of liberty only at his own level. We who are more responsible at our cultural level, however, could consider ourselves irresponsible. The disorder of the world is not primarily the outcome of real sin, a clear-sighted will to evil; it is primarily the outcome of ignorance, imprudence, and human stupidity. But isn't real sin present there—the sin of a responsible being capable of wisdom, reflection, education—that unconscious sin that makes us unconsciously commit these stupidities, these follies?

Everything is quasi-unconscious and irresponsible, but the evil is no less enormous for that. Who could appraise the responsibility of that psychopath Hitler and those following him, mentally ill themselves, or hypnotized? The catastrophic human weakness (due to the corporeal conditions of man's origin) that makes the temptation to fall easier than the vocation to climb, the bad use of self easier than the good use—isn't this original sin, rather than a fall from a state of perfection necessarily entailing progress? This necessity of progress is part of man's nature, which is made for social progress from savagery to civilization; but if the progress be deflected in an incoherent fashion through the course of a bloody and barbarous history, a Way of the Cross of wars and revolutions, isn't this confirmation that man behaves badly, consciously or otherwise, proof that he is in a state of original inadequacy which, in a being capable of reflection and of good, may justly be classed as a state of original sin?

Science tells us that the Adam of science was by no means in a state of cultural perfection; yet it is a mistake to say the same of the Adam of faith. If a man, even a primitive man, is in a state of grace, and behaves rightly—which means corresponding to his aptitudes, it is a sign that he is obeying his nature and God and is therefore open to grace. On the other hand, if he conducts himself badly, even with the attenuated responsibility of primitive man, he is still cutting himself off from grace through infidelity to God. This is what the dogma of original sin implies: not some unimaginable perfection of man, but a primitive man in a state of grace, who is thus immensely superior to the intellectual technocrats. Adam, an old peasant full of correct intuitions, is much more authentic than an agricultural expert—which is not to say that the (really indispensable) agricultural technology is bad, only that it should not overrule the peasant's correct intuitions but rather seek to give them explicit form.

And so if we—believers or unbelievers—understand it correctly as the perversion of the man who makes up his mind according to his own idea of good and evil without allowing for the promptings of his nature, original sin should suggest to us not a fall from a utopian state of perfection through the single sin of one man alone, but the state of *human inadequacy* through failure to reflect on what cuts man off from his nature (which is his vocation). Sound theology has never told us that Adam was deprived of the warning and protective equipment that physical suffering provides, has never denied his biological death. The perversion of original sin takes form in insufficient

self-control and clear-sightedness, and this makes physical
suffering unendurable (the very thing that is overcome in natural childbirth) and winces in anguish at the thought of the
normal change of state that takes place at death.

It is classical Protestantism that overestimates the perverse-
ness of original sin, on the ground that it is necessary to debase
man before God, since God saves us to a certain extent in spite
of ourselves. On the other hand, Catholic theology—if not all
Catholics, and certainly not the "integrists"—has had the merit
of reconciling original sin with a respect for a human nature
that becomes merely more difficult to discover and to follow. To
be fully natural, man needs to be saved. And he will always
have this need.

For a scientist a striking confirmation of original sin is that
although man may concede the objective rationality of good,
which is sane and healthy, he will always, absurdly enough, find
it more tempting to give himself over to evil. This is illogical
and stupid and it indicates original inadequacy in contradis-
tinction to the real vocation of man. To believe, as so many
Marxists do, that abolishing capitalist alienation of man would
lead to the utopia of a new golden age—namely, a classless
society—is a serious mistake, for man, however freed from alienation and educated he may be, will always be tempted by
the mindlessness and stupidity of a dehumanized and dehumanizing technocracy that has no sanctions. Thus we can dem-
onstrate that man, a limited being, inadequate and weak, will
always have need of God.

To man lost in evil the cross is offered; but he wants no part
of it for he neither wishes to suffer unjustly nor does he wish the
Just One to suffer. Though the Apostles were shocked and
rebellious, the legions of angels did not intervene, for the suffering of the Just One was necessary, unless He were not the Just
One at all but a god of pride and of triumph.

What was Christ incarnated to do if not to allow God to take on our weakness through the free fiat of the Virgin Mary? Mary was the only fully free woman, and this meant to her that being recognized as immaculate was not a protective privilege but rather a recognition of a state. She was the person who always said No to evil and Yes to God in full liberty and without being constrained either way. (Her opposite is Eve, who said Yes to evil and No to good, without being constrained to, and had the foolishness, like all of us, to put herself into a state of original sin.) But isn't it utopian, men being what they are, to believe that the Incarnation could have been other than redemptive, or could have avoided its culmination of the cross? We are asked to take up our cross with Christ, and we resist, forgetting that our cross is our situation, human and weak, and that by his incarnation Christ has automatically assumed our situation, and has thus demonstrated the true meaning of the cross, which is to make the humanizing effort *to lift it.*

The actual cross of Calvary was only the logical conclusion of the Incarnation in a world given over to evil. But it succeeds in showing the love of God, since "greater love than this no man hath, that a man lay down his life for his friends." While this has its profound place in theology it is still a matter of a very simple truth. Taking on the human condition, God showed that it was possible to save oneself by lifting up the cross of original stupidity—the outcome of original inadequacy. But because God exalts love to the degree of becoming our model, frail yet victorious, through His own weakness and His very death He teaches us to make use of the evil of our frailty in order to bring good out of it. This is the natural aspect of the Redemption. The justification of what is so appalling in evolution and in history is not only the fact of human liberty; it is as much the fact that human nature could be united to the divine nature in Christ at a moment of human history, a moment that might appear to be contingent but was nonetheless crucial, the climacteric, the point of no return.

We have now a *model of a perfect man* that is particularly useful to us. In order to be truly men, faithful to their nature-vocation, we are now interested in practicing the *imitation of Jesus Christ, the ideal image of man,* normal perfect man, our prototype—whether or not we believe in His divinity. But if we are afraid to aim so high as to imitate the Man-God, the Catholic Church, which does not believe in debasing God in raising man, offers a model closer to us, a woman among all women, the Virgin Mary.

Unfortunately we seem to incline either to mariolatry or to mariophobia, and we do not understand the vital wisdom of referring ourselves to the virginity of Mary. Whereas, the most important thing is not, as we think, the divine paternity of Christ confirmed by the anatomical virginity, it is the *spirit of virginity* of Mary; and this is the grace of expendability, of understanding, the grace of being unfettered and detached. These are all qualities we laboriously try to acquire through psychophysical methods of relaxation; yet Mary seemed to have them of herself, thus plainly confirming that she was the new, and immaculate, Eve. This was not simply because she was anatomically a virgin but because she had the spirit of virginity, the spirit of purity, which she offers for our example, whatever be our state, married or celibate.

The cross we carry is the burden of our nature. But we should not languidly drift into sensual pleasure, instead of playing our role, which is to save ourselves—that is, to take up our cross and accept its more positive meaning as an instrument of progress. We develop naturally by means of the cross of our nature. But because God assumed the human condition and the cross, the Redemption effortfully took on its full significance: that of the return of man to his vocation and to God. God has loved us to that extreme, which is not simply the relation of an autonomizing and liberating Creation, but is actual participation as exemplar in our condition, with its difficulties and its glories. As men we cannot be dispensed from the human condition that bears its cross; through imitation of Jesus Christ, however, we are in a position to make good use of our condition to go forward—we and our fellow men—in the direction of true progress.

In the natural sense human inadequacy, the source of the sin, was even before Christ an instrument of progress in the struggle against this oppressive burden. As the result of the redemptive incarnation of God in Christ, it becomes an instrument of salvation not merely natural but supernatural as well.

Promised Eternity

But the love of God, the creator of a free nature, is not limited to utilizing inadequacies in order to turn them into instruments of progress. God's love consists in giving to creation—this evolutionary adventure in matter, this daughter of time—its full meaning by carrying its fulfillment into eternity. What, we wonder dejectedly, is all this that is not eternal? It does seem paradoxical that man should develop up to extreme old age and then that all this maturation process should be climaxed by disappearing in death.

To ripen is to die. Suppose our only consolation were the stoic acceptance of our mortal nature and the joy of having shared to the utmost in the human effort. But isn't even that effort destined to follow the lot of our earth—that is, to disappear? Is it sensible to think that science will succeed in rescuing man from his mortal nature, even if it succeeds in postponing accidental death or death from old age? Is it sensible to hope that, from planet to planet, through cosmonautical adventure, humanity and its culture will fight a delaying action in the face of inevitable disappearance?

We know that Christian Revelation vouches for what is called the immortality of the soul. What is more: man cannot disappear in his spiritual essence. Science, which knows only the spirit in its incarnate, corporeal state, could not object to this. Science is satisfied to find in the Christian hypothesis of immortality an assuagement of the scandal of old age. While affirming the difference of psychobiological nature in man and animal, science is happy to see confirmation of this theory in the difference in metaphysical nature of the informing principle giving to the body its human complexity.

Although immortality is thought impossible, we could not have a genuine capacity for reflection if the ego were carnal only and not the incarnation of a spirit—and about this spirit rational philosophy tells us (even before revealed faith assures us of it) that since it is simple it is indestructible and cannot die.

But Christianity goes even farther, promising eternity to both matter and flesh and rescuing them from this destiny of death on another plane of being: a more complete and tenable materialism. This belief in immortality holds true on the individual plane, where it is propounded in what is called the resurrection of the flesh, or better, the *glorification* of man. The resurrection of the flesh seems to have inspired the painters' depiction of the dead leaving their tombs. This is clearly an impossibility, since for the most part the corpses would have long since disappeared, their elements having been assimilated by other beings.

Still it is wrong to poke fun at this. What is really involved is that the soul resumes its role of *informing* what looks like similar matter but is actually incorruptible matter, since it has crossed over into glorification. Since incorruptible matter is not an object of scientific study, science can give no description of it; but this does not at all prove that it does not exist. Thus, for the materialist, it is an interesting twist that Christian survival is not an ideal inimical to matter.

Christianity does not stop with individual immortality, however. In fact it is explicitly with immortality that Christianity deals. And long before Teilhard with his grounding in modern science, St. Paul was singing mystically of the *glorification of the cosmos:* the new heavens and the new earth, the celestial Jerusalem. And this Christian belief, based on Revelation, is in agreement with the ambiguity of the world's thermodynamic destiny to which Teilhard directs our attention.

Physics tends to emphasize the dissipation and exhaustion of usable energy pushing us inexorably toward thermal death at the absolute zero: the disappearance of all activity. But while everything is being dissipated, biology shows us a sector of life where, by use of the laws of thermodynamics, progress is being achieved. This progress derives from organization that is form-giving and opposed to entropy. Is such an ascent by means of decline to be arrested one day through exhaustion of energy? Or shall we emerge on to a new threshold, the step of glorifica-tion, the reflection of energy in which the cosmos, abandoning matter doomed to death, will be transfigured? Science is silent. Religion affirms it.

Thus, in the purview of true Christianity, man was not exiled in this valley of tears to obtain through suffering the immortality of his soul in a heaven that has nothing to do with this earth. He comes upon the earth in order to accomplish here, by dint of hard labor, a work of individual and commu-nal development, nothing of which will be lost. It is to the extent of our effectiveness here on earth that death will settle us in a condition called heaven or hell that is neither reward nor punishment but simply the confirmation of what we did. We must not look at this from the naturalistic point of view and maintain that it is the human work that will be glorified. At the end of time the human task, like each one of us at the close of our existence, is destined to be confronted by God-love—that is, by Fire. Everything will be consumed. Hence we should en-deavor to make ourselves and our work a good fuel that the

Fire-love will transform into an element of the eternal city, for otherwise the evil fuel will fire the alienated, evil "flames" of hell.

Which one thinks more highly of matter: the materialist who, in order to preserve his total autonomy, tells us that it is absurd, an ephemeral adventure, or the spiritual Christian who gives it this dimension of eternity by proclaiming it to be the free daughter of God?

Thus God-love, for whom creation is a work of love and who came because of love to share in our destiny, calls us to a human task, the vocation of being co-creators of a terrestrial city destined to be transcended in a city of God. And by way of giving us more energy and more understanding, He not only gives himself to us in Christ as the prototype of normal man; He gives himself to us also through the *material* means of nourishment under the form of the food of love where He is mysteriously present, the Eucharist.

This is not a memorial, not a symbol, but a spiritual presence, and something infinitely more: a real presence, whose transubstantiation (to use the theological concept seeking to explain it rationally) still suggests the word "scandalous" that was heard when the formula, "This is my body. . . . Whenever you do this, you will do it in memory of me," was first heard. Are we going to walk away, uncomprehending and scandalized? Or, like the Apostles, shall we remain faithful without understanding the mystery, inasmuch the One who speaks to us cannot deceive us?

Made to Love God

Thus it is that man is lovable, since God, the Creator and Redeemer, loves him to this degree. But can man truly *love* God? For after all, man knows the unknowable only insofar as it is revealed to him. It is by *being love*—that is, by *amoriza-*

tion—that man plays his part and proves that he is living in the love of God. And he credits this love not to his own unaided efforts but to fidelity to his nature and vocation and grace from God. It is by prompting him to persevere in the development of his nature, and by giving him the graces for this fidelity that God causes him to accomplish the works of salvation *within the faith*. It is the faith that saves, to be sure; but it is inseparable from the works.

But the complete man is not simply the one who loves his fellows (necessary though this is) and collaborates with them in the social and political work of building a society of love. The complete man believes, knows, feels God to be a Person with whom he is able to entertain personal loving relations. Not only can he do this, he *must*. The neurophysiology of self-love and love of others gives us the threefold cerebral hierarchy. We find it here again when we question scientifically how God loves us and how we can love Him in return. (This inquiry, of course, presupposes belief in Him; but it also shows the natural value of this belief, its possibility, its probability.)

The personal God loves us as a person, since the goal of evolution has been to lead matter up precisely to this stage where individuality supports the personal being who is capable of relations no longer indirect, as between Creator and unconscious creature, but direct, as between father and child. This Father is the prototype of the father who knows how to remain a father while guiding his child to liberty, a Father in whom there is so little of the tyrant that His respect for us led Him even to the sacrifice of the cross. In the love of God all types of human relations are to be seen in their perfection and imitated on our own plane. The riches of the Trinity, which are observed better than they are rationally expressed, offer us in analogy the love of the fatherly Creator; the brotherly love of Christ, a man like us who is the word and who teaches us to pray; and, finally, all the wealth of the passion of love without the temptations of the flesh lie in our relations with the Holy Spirit.

As we have seen, in us love is the consciousness of our existence, of our ego and of its needs, the consciousness of the existence of others and of the need for exchanges with them for our own personal growth. Love is the affectionate consciousness of a presence: our own and that of others; an existence where one *is,* but is not alone. It is similar with the love of God, for He is at one and the same time God in us, the presence of His presence and of His person, and the unconscious need we have of Him.

The presence in us of the Creator, He who is the real cause of our existence, above and beyond all the mechanisms of the ego—implies a human, emotional, intellectual relation with this presence, the image and idea of God in us. It is at our threefold cerebral level that this relation with God comes into play, like the relation with ourselves and with others.

It is primarily through His presence in us that we love God, in the religious feeling that makes us dimly conscious of this intimate and secret presence at the very heart of our flesh, a need of this instinct for God we can misunderstand just as we can misunderstand our social instinct. It is a very natural and spontaneous personal feeling, and stronger than the ego or the feeling for others in relation to ourselves and what we are, since we are made for such a relation. Made by God, made for God, we have in us the need of God, and this need is an emotional attraction. To argue that religion is more than feeling is not to infer something so rational that it is devoid of feeling.

But by virtue of Revelation, which fills in the inadequacies of our reason, and because of the existence of Christ, our neotic brain not only can be conscious of the religious need but can also rationalize this need into a sure knowledge of God, so that He is no longer an obscure presence but a person with whom dialogue is possible.

Yet believing is more than merely feeling and thinking. There is a superior dimension transcending these two: the dimension of interpersonal contact, a loving involvement established by means of the prefrontal brain between the innermost reach of our soul and the divine Person. The brain that cares for the future, the brain that can perceive an ideal, is made for loving relations with an ideal that is not abstract but a real person. We need a relation with a person who is not like other persons. So we seek to create such a relation by making idols for ourselves—that is, by putting in God's place someone who is not God; when we do this we deceive and imbalance ourselves; and if the idol is a human being we deceive and unbalance him. Human relations must remain at the level that respects equality within complementarity. Yet man is so made that he needs unequal relations, needs to enter into relations with a superior who is not an oppressor, needs to know that he, a limited being, carnal and mortal, is in relation with an Absolute who is a person.

It is not by inventing God to compensate for his wretchedness that man becomes alienated; it is by trying to become God or by making idols of the values or the injustices of this world. The Marxist statement that a non-alienated man in a classless society would have no further need of God is simply utopian. He will still be man, a limited being, and he will retain this need of an Absolute which he is not. The important point to decide is whether because of the so justly criticized false images of God and of the evil consequences they produce in human affairs, all religious formation—that is, the possibility of attaining to the true God, which requires *the teaching of Revelation*—should be forbidden. This crucial point the dialogue between believers and unbelievers must settle.

Unbelievers are too ready to see confirmation that God does not exist in the fact that faith requires investigation and study, for this they look upon as a conditioning and brainwashing. As a matter of fact, man must be taught everything. Man must learn to love God, just as he must learn what is good for him and why he must love others. Hence it is a mistake to hold that one should reach adulthood before making up one's mind in religious matters, so that the child will not come under any influence. Once the child has become an adult, he must assume an adult religion by adopting in adult fashion the faith of his childhood, but from the earliest moment of his consciousness he must learn how to enter into a relation with the God he needs. This in no way invalidates the liberty of his future choice.

Apprenticeship in the relation with God is the whole object of the religious life. It is the long labor of the mystic who in the "dark night" strips himself of false images in order to reach the Other. It is the quest for a love beyond feeling or words. True mysticism is to be found not in spectacular and questionable phenomena, but in renunciation and the purity of an authentic contact between God and the most intimate point of our incarnate soul. It is the consciousness of a silence full of presence and tenderness.

The way there is the same as that for enhancing our love of self and neighbor; it lies in relaxation, source of understanding and interior peace that teaches us to will without the conscious effort of willing. One cannot encounter God in a state of agitation and nervous exhaustion. Thus the hygienic quest for calm leads to God, while the quest for God presupposes health of brain and health of soul. Convents and monasteries, far from seeming to be obsolete preserves where men and women are exposed to dehumanization through excesses or mortification and asceticism, appear to an ever greater degree to be havens of peace and calm of which we shall have ever more need.

Prayer, as Père Daniélou says, is becoming a political problem; that is, the political power has the duty to provide the conditions for prayer since they are the conditions of human balance as well. But for asceticism to be humanizing, its necessity and limits must be understood. Poverty, chastity, and obedience are not mortifications that diminish us; they are in fact conditions of the growth of self in the struggle against egoism. It is not only Zen Buddhism or Hindu Yoga that have emphasized the liaison between the physical and the spiritual. Within the Christian context, indeed, these methods could be even more self-expanding, for the Christian knows that it is not a question of his becoming de-personalized through losing himself in an anonymous whole, but rather one of "super-personalizing" himself in the contact with a personal God. And he will be doing this not in order to forget others but in order to serve them better (See J. M. Dechanet, *La Voie du silence* [Paris, 1963] on this matter.)

In fact all types of Christian spirituality, when stripped of Manichean and Jansenist error, emerge as the art of living more perfectly by making better use of the brain's potentialities—but only if one sees in original sin not the impossibility of acting rightly but rather the obligation to try harder to relax and submit to the grace of God, who demands our active participation. Training in cerebral control allows one to pray better, but praying better compels one to learn self-control. This is something very well understood by Dr. Vittoz. As he writes,

"A sense of God is worth more than the idea of God. One must first of all be receptive: to open oneself up in order to receive. One must forget self, be open, keep silent, empty oneself so that God may possess the whole soul and that there may be nothing other than Him. One must pray with the heart and not with the head; learn how to achieve silence in oneself, to open in order to receive. But we must know how to wait, how to dispose ourselves simply to receive what we cannot give to ourselves. We are receiving even when we feel nothing. For you who believe in the Real Presence, how great is the moment of receiving Holy Communion! How essential it is to keep silent then, to open oneself, to forget oneself, to empty oneself so that

God may possess the whole being, so that there will be nothing
other than Him. Humility is not debasing: before God it is
consoling to feel one's lowliness and to know that one is loved."

The significance of Christianity lies in the Incarnation,
which has brought God nearer to man without lowering Him.
To pray is to imitate Jesus Christ, it is to pray Jesus Christ.
God's love is no longer an abstraction, it is the love of the
Christ of the Gospel for all men. It is expressed distinctively in
the symbol of the Sacred Heart dear to Père de Foucauld, but a
symbol Père Teilhard has shown to be not a sentimental
expression of religiosity but the heart of religion: at the heart
of the world the heart of a God.

Humanity, The Mystical Body of Christ

But the incarnation has still a greater significance. It means
not only that we have an exemplary Man to imitate, one who,
being God, gives a redemptive value to the Cross rightly carried, and gives us the graces we need. It concerns not only our
individual salvation but also our personal salvation, which is to
say that it comes about not in the solitude of dialogue with God
but in human solidarity.

Christ is not Man-God among men: He is God *belonging to
humanity,* the salvation of humanity as humanity. We have
seen that the command to love one's neighbor as oneself does
not stop at private social relations but extends to public life as
well. It is out of the question to think that one loves while
tolerating social injustices "justified" by the laws of economics. Such social institutions must be humanized and personalized so that they may become institutions of love. When
Teilhard thus proposes the upbuilding of the society of man's
development, the noosphere, he is helped in his sociological
reflections by his Christian faith, for this yields the prototype of
such a society. By becoming incarnate, Christ has become the

Head of humanity, as is expressed in the teachings of the Mystical Body, of the Communion of Saints, and of Vicarious Atonement. We are not isolated individuals, attached only to God. We form a body growing from generation to generation in a "Christogenesis" that adds nothing to Christ but brings more members to the Head.

The Christian, then, is not simply one who imitates Jesus Christ but more: one who participates in the life of a kind of organism of which He is the head, who receives life from the Head, and all of whose actions are important not only for himself but for the entire organism. As St. Paul warns, do not by your actions take the members of Jesus Christ and make them members of a harlot.

Unfortunately the doctrine of the Mystical Body was superseded by the "People of God" concept before it had taken its rightful place in our lives.[1] It remains outside our ordinary life, a part of our spiritual life that we persist in withholding from the secular life. The Mystical Body is the Church; it is our relation with the dead. We do not realize that this is a question of all humanity, that secular society is the body of Christ and that for that reason, its viciousness should be a scandal for the Christian.

This does not mean confusing the natural with the supernatural; it does mean not keeping them apart. Christ does not reign as king in the unjust way of the kings of this earth. Yet He is the true King. The Christian is not of the world, which is condemned; but this world, which is condemned, is the world of injustice; and to be not of this world is to strive to build the true world, which approximates not the world of Satan but the world of God.

---

1. Interpolation by Editor. Author states merely that the Pauline doctrine has not been realized, "despite Pope Pius XII, despite Teilhard." Actually it is a casualty of the new biblical theology, which finds "People of God" richer in meaning and of course more venerable.—*Ed.*

To confuse civil society and the Mystical Body is to fall into the error of clericalism and to ignore the necessity for technical competence on the part of the economist or the politician; it is to approve—the height of intolerance—the idea of a state religion. Yet to separate them amounts to the opposite error of laicism, for this removes the social, economic, and political institutions from their essential element, their term of reference. Then the technician becomes a technocrat who ignores man. It is not necessary to be a believer to labor for the betterment of human affairs; but the values of love are too much misunderstood today, and the technocratic and Existentialist dangers are too great for anyone to think he can dispense with the Christian contribution.

The religion of love was made to teach us love, and if it does so while remaining faithful to its own authenticity it can avoid both confusion and alienation. The important thing always is not to confound the immanent and the transcendent but not to separate them either. The Christian should appreciate the common natural values while at the same time vindicating them supernaturally. He relates love to God, but he does not impose love in the name of God, nor God in the name of love; his faith helps him to see more plainly the conditions of love at the heart of the world and not solely and entirely in a transcendent way outside the world.

The Christian does not replace socio-economic techniques with theology, but he directs those techniques so that secular society may conform with what its religious dimension as the Mystical Body expects of it. Thus he labors to shape a society devoted to the service of human betterment, while at the same time refuting by his own involvement those just criticisms of the lack of interest in earthly things shown by Christians interested only in heaven. This is one of the principal arguments of atheism. In a world without love the real revolution is the reintroduction of love—that is, making social justice rule, but through the community and not through bureaucracy.

The insistence upon the social dimension of man, which is achieved by a continuously extended socialization, may lead some people to fear a totalitarianism that will stifle the human personality. There is undoubtedly a danger here: we see many examples of it. True, man is becoming increasingly the slave of social, economic, and political structures that were made for his service rather than he for their service. Economists and politicians are not wicked; yet they end by perpetrating or at least tolerating positive wrongs in the name of the "laws" of "human" science, laws that are evidently becoming ever more inhuman. Economic development or financial interest come before human interests. *Love of man must be put back into the government of human affairs.* Man's well-being must not be imposed on him, but he must be helped to achieve it himself in freedom.

The leader is in danger of being imbalanced by his power, as the spectacular example of Stalin shows so well. This, however, is to be explained not only by the character of Stalin but also by the facts that the dictatorship of the proletariat is the dictatorship of the leaders of the proletariat and that a dictator cannot be normal any more than can those subjected to his dictatorship. This is not peculiar to any specific regime but is to be found among all leaders when they are cut off from a community whose free communal decisions they express. True democracy consists not in delegating its powers to those who, imbalanced by their pseudo-superiority, take over the role of leadership, but in the permanent collaboration between leaders and people on political decisions in the common interest.

When Teilhard proposes the noosphere the question of the danger of a depersonalizing totalitarianism is raised. This would be a real danger if the noosphere were a super-individual, which is not the case. The noosphere would not be the noosphere if it tolerated the dictatorship of a technocratic leader. An organism needs direction. Teilhard as a Christian

shows us then that the head of the noosphere exists, indeed; but
it is Christ, the head of the Mystical Body, a personal God not
at all tempted to become oppressive or depersonalizing. It is
obedience to the Head that ensures the freedom of the Christian in the face of all oppressions.

If only Christians labored with professional efficiency to
make a world worthy of their Head, Christ, unbelievers could
find no difficulty with what they were doing, for this would fall
in the area of man's development and of the struggle against
injustice. Yet paradoxically we see how often Christians practice
their Christianity badly, considering only their individual salvation and their relations with a remote God, from the standpoint of another world and without much feeling for this one.
In fact they not only distort its nature but make it absolutely
uninviting for unbelievers as well.

The precept of love then ceases to be an essential for our
development, both individual and communal (as it must be if
we are to be able to *love in God*) ; it seems to be not love at all,
or at any rate a bad kind of love. To love in God is to become
wholly immersed in the divine milieu that is the energy of love.
It is to love like God, with God's love, with a deferential
tenderness; it is to be an *active transmitter of love within the
Mystical Body*. In this way the just hierarchy of human values
is restored. The people most effective in this are not the most
powerful or learned, corrupted as they may be by egoism and
pride; it is the ordinary, the humble (i.e., those who have the
spirit of poverty, who ask to be poor, not those destroyed by
destitution) , those who know the value of love.

On the natural plane, contrary to what is often thought,
those who are ill and infirm are more human, more normal
than those in good health, since for them to strive to be as
normal as possible despite everything requires great effort that
we should be wrong to think useless. So we should realize how
much truer this must be in the spiritual-communal perspective

that vivifies the full meaning of suffering and weakness for us and others in a world corrupted by egoism. Not that we should love suffering and illness with a neurotic dolefulness (for in excess they are dehumanizing); but they do keep us aware of our limited and frail nature. They are crosses and they are redemptive, in the measure that we accept them—that is, far from being senselessly defiant, we try to lift them so that, growing with true greatness, we make love grow. And in this we follow the Head of the Mystical Body, who made of the cross an instrument of salvation and thus gave a positive meaning even to what would otherwise seem to suggest only diminution and dissolution.

It is not only space that separates men and is overcome in the Mystical Body; it is time as well. This passing time, which destroys and consumes us, is not simply the condition of maturing for another world where time will no longer be—at least in the sense that progress necessitates destruction. Time, the creature of God, is not separated from eternity, its absolute. In the divine milieu everything is present, so that we are assured of actual coexistence with the past and with the future: direct beneficiaries in God in this fusion with all humanity. To love the dead is not simply to recall them in the past and to pray for them while imagining them elsewhere; rather, it is to know that they remain united to us in the same community but occupying another place. Gone from our space-time, which is our clothing of flesh, they are not farther away than our most remote contemporaries, for love, the fabric of the world, obliterates distances, and everything becomes close. (See on this topic the scientific reflections of the physicist Olivier Costa de Beauregard, *Le Second principe de la science du temps* [Paris, 1963].)

Christianity and Progress

Now this organism of superpersonalization is not only growing numerically; it is developing in quality as well. Through its agency men are continuing the *amorization* of the world in its movement from the multiple to the one. And this human task is not an ephemeral one, but is destined, like ourselves, for "glorification."

In defining clearly the full meaning of this human task, in showing us what genuine human progress is—the true values we enjoy not when we receive them ready-made but discover and make our own—Christianity emerges as essential to the modern world, for it is the *religion of progress.* It is such both in itself and in its dogmatic theology, for its work of intensifying and deepening our understanding of Revelation will never end. The dogmas do not change, but we can keep formulating them better. Because it is a religion of tradition, Catholicism is by that very fact a religion of progress, since tradition is merely an added deposit of truth that must be taken into account because it is recognized as authentic.

For the modern world of science and technology, Teilhard, in his union of science and faith, is the apostle of true progress, for he witnesses to love in the optimism of the cross. Yet it would be a pity to forget his real precursor, the biologist Dr. Philippe J. B. Buchez, who along with Frédéric Ozanam was one of the great thinkers and militant social Christians of the 19th century, but is now grossly underrated. Although Dr. Buchez died almost a century before Teilhard (in 1865), he was a leading exponent of the belief that Christianity is a religion of progress, a revolutionary religion. While he regretted that the Christian world had advanced little in this direction, he remained sure of his belief, and in a certain sense anticipated the times of Pope John XXIII for, with the disappearance of the temporal power of the Papacy, he foresaw that the Pope might well become the spiritual counselor of the whole world.

In the parliamentary history of the French Revolution of which he was co-author, he shows that the great revolutionary principles of liberty, equality, and fraternity are Christian principles and that the Revolution failed because it was not animated by Christianity. Committed to the service of the poor in the struggle against laissez-faire capitalism and revolutionary political action, and founder of the French Carbonari, Dr. Buchez himself had become an atheist. In his enthusiasm for biology, however, he discovered evolution for himself, and saw in a thorough-going hygiene the basis for a morality of human betterment. And toward 1825, as with Teilhard, he found his thinking on evolution leading him to God, as well as to a conviction of the existence and necessity for morality. Like Teilhard, he saw in social progress the springboard to another plane of biological progress. It was Saint-Simon's final work, *The New Christianity* (which he had read in 1825), that convinced him that not a new Christianity but true Christianity was needed as a doctrine of progress. Opposing the disciples of Saint-Simon, now immersed in pantheism, he turned toward Catholicism as being progressive and revolutionary. About 1840 he wrote his *Traité complet de philosophie du point de vue du catholicisme et du progrès,* culminating in his *Traité de politique et de science sociale,* which appeared after his death in 1866.

As his disciple A. Ott wrote in his appreciation, "All Buchez's teaching rests upon the idea of progress. . . . His predecessors had seen only the purely human side of progress. They had established the perfectibility of the individual and of society. Buchez understood that progress is the general law of the world. A pioneer, in fact, he related the progressive facts established by the historic sciences, from analogous results provided by comparative anatomy, geology, and embryogeny, and established a general relation between the laws of inorganic, organic, and spiritual nature. . . . The progressive character does not reside in each isolated term of the series, but in the general nature of the series itself, in the relation of the terms with one another. . . .

"If progress is the general law of the world, it follows that nothing here on earth was created for itself, but that on the contrary all things have for their purpose to fulfill a function in the universal order, to do a work whose dimensions infinitely surpass that of their own existence. . . . Man does not differ in this regard from beings inferior to him, except in that in fulfilling his function it is not sufficient for him to follow blindly the blind impulses of his organism; in that the work he must accomplish is contained in a law proposed to his intelligence—the moral law; and in that in obeying this law he is freely carrying out his function in the universal order—and with full knowledge of the reason.

The general principle of modern civilization is Christianity. . . . It teaches (in effect) the communal interdependence of all men as members of a society that is the human species; it summons all men. . . . It lays down as a principle their moral unity; their fraternity; their equal right to reward or punishment—that is to say, their liberty. It lays down as duties compassion for the poor, protection for the weak, and charity amid all—charity, *caritas*, which is something much more than love. It holds up moral superiority before all men as a primary good, and ability . . . as something to be put to the profit of all men. . . . The word "progress" does not occur in the Gospel; but the idea is there, and there it represents not only individual perfection but also a general purpose. . . .

"All these principles are laid down as goals to be attained. I am summing them up in these words, which I repeat: the thorough and entire emancipation of the human species. . . . The socialist aspirations of 1848, which were themselves so attacked and so feared whatever their origin and under whatever false colors, represented no more than the thousands of such attempts proposed or tried out in earlier centuries by Christian charity. . . . For a religion to become extinct it must be in contradiction to the movement of civilization or progress. No one can say that of Christianity. Its presence is necessary in order to give to certain principles—accepted by politics, though far from being realized—their value as truth and their meaning, as, for instance, the doctrine of fraternity. Furthermore, all that Christianity proposes has not as yet even reached the state of a simple desideratum in politics. . . . Modern civilization is born of Christianity. . . . The destinies of Christianity and those of future civilization are inseparable.

"This earthly life—so tormented, so mingled with good and bad—which we suffer for a few years, is explained to us by the doctrine of progress. It is a task we are accomplishing between the past and the future. . . . Our life is no longer a dead work emerging from the slime of the morning to return there in the evening, and rumbling blindly on into the gloomy shades of matter. No, it moves freely, in the broad daylight of the Spirit under the eye of Him who has given it a task so that it might exist. We are not alone on this earth, without anyone who understands us and has loved and does love us. Every effort of ours, however small, however paltry it may be, is of some value and service; it is received and counted. Reasoning and knowledge—they are a dedication. Error and fatuity—they are simply egoism. The whole logic of the universe, its very soul, so to speak, is enclosed within the word *progress*.

"Christianity did not come solely to purify and to perfect the individual life. It came to set forth a *political* theology as well. To be convinced of the truth of this statement one has only to admit that a religion has to govern societies as well as individuals."

And Dr. Buchez shows how Christianity, when it appeared, humanized the institutions of the ancient world and so transformed them.

MATTER AND MYSTERY

Conclusion

SHOULD WE BE OPTIMISTIC or pessimistic when we contemplate this world of ours? Obviously, when we consider the wonderful triumphs of science and technology we must feel optimistic. To be plunged into pessimism, on the other hand, all we have to do is ponder the unutterable misery to be found in the same world where money is squandered for war or the conquest of the moon. Will it not all come inexorably to an evil end, especially in view of the terrible powers of destruction that science has put into our hands? We are no longer at the turn of

the 2oth century, when everyone believed that scientific progress and education would inevitably bring about moral and
human progress. Must we then in all honesty be pessimists? Not
at all.

In company with God on the Seventh Day we can say that the
world is good; but we are not yet at Man's seventh day, when it
will be time for us to rest because the days will be accomplished
and we shall enter into glory. Such as it is and as it must be
kept, the world is not good in itself; it is as good as its aptitudes,
and insofar as it is a *machine for progress.* It is the world's
natural and normal destiny to perfect itself, to improve itself;
but this does not happen of its own accord. We are in the time
of man, and it is up to man either to make his potentialities
available to the world, or to destroy them.

Optimism was justified in a pre-human world where, in spite
of the failures, an undoubted ascent took place; but when it
comes to the future of a world that is in man's hands, then
everything depends on him. But is man good or is he evil? We
know how philosophers have discussed this question, emphasizing the good in man and the evil in society or the other way
around—as though social evil could be anything other than an
inadequacy in individuals, an inadequacy that makes society
evil and unwholesome.

Like the world, man is "naturally" good; but here again it is
only an aptitude for good that still has to be deliberately and
freely realized. We shall be good only when we are taught to be
so and prevented from growing up any old way in an evil
milieu. As science confirms, this naturally good man is a naturally weak being: fragile, prey to numerous natural temptations to denaturalization. And science, as we have recalled, is
not so far from the theological thesis of original sin rightly
understood.

Man is not primarily a being who does evil: he is a being

capable of discerning good from evil but doing evil without even adverting to it, since he acts without reflecting. *Homo sapiens,* naturally intelligent man, behaves as though he were naturally stupid.

So the dilemma between optimism and pessimism comes back to this: Will man, with his aptitude for good, be capable of overcoming his appalling lack of reflection, his negligence, his imprudence, his ignorance? Will he who has two eyes ever be able to open them to see what he is doing and the consequences of his deeds? Man follows only his own inclination, and his inclination is a monstrous egoistic pride that would cause him (if it had the power to) to destroy the world rather than change his ideas. The powerful of the world are confronted only by those they have subdued; and they in their turn dream of becoming tyrants themselves; and, while awaiting the fulfillment of their ambition, practice tyranny within the modest limits of such power as they have. Meanwhile the truly humble people have fled the world in order to atone through penance and mortification in a way not understood by the world, but yet a way that is, in their very struggle against egoism, the secret of human betterment.

If the world is to succeed by human effort, man must understand where his blindness is leading him, must realize what his job is and that it is not easy at best. Man will not owe his success to the automatisms of ascent, nor to the furtherance of a freedom that is unable to make decisions, nor to the use of drugs that allow him to behave badly without too many ill effects. He will owe it to his awareness of the good and his will to do it without balking at the normal difficulty of seeing the good and doing it. But he will not do good if it is imposed upon him as a law whose justification he does not understand.

To the man who is genuinely interested not only in his own good (albeit he has not understood what it is) it must be pointed out that, being what he is, his good must necessarily involve the good of others, and this means the good of all humanity.

To make man aware of what he *is* is the most urgent of all tasks. The man who dreads the thought of action must be persuaded that the secret of action lies in preliminary control, and that the secret of control lies not in effort but in relaxation, the source of a clear mind and interior peace. We have within us the power to reflect, but in order to use it we must be taught to control our brain instead of yielding to its automatisms. Then we can see why we cannot will whatever we like according to our whims, but only the good that is our good, the good without which we should lose our liberty. To reflect is to guide ourselves by referring to the norm of whatever moves us to act in conformity with it.

Christian morality lays before us as a rule of life that we love our neighbor as ourselves. Today neurophysiology confirms that this is actually the law of balance of our being also, and does so by defining this love that informs our person, that marvelous individuality that emerges from organic integrations and social interrelations.

For things to go right with the world it is enough for man to observe the psychomatic hygiene that obliges him to love himself properly for his own balance, his own good health, and his own development. But this he cannot do if he does not love others by collaborating with them in the human task of the betterment of humanity.

We want to be happy. The only happiness lies in *knowing how to love,* which is the technique of happiness. Knowing how to use the matter that is our flesh, not letting it crush us under its weight but, in view of its vocation, making it the vehicle of our ascent.

Since we are beings constituted by the bond of love we can live only in and through love; but if we can apparently satisfy ourselves with a surrogate for love, that will be merely an apparent satisfaction, for true balance, true peace, true happiness are found only in conforming with what we are.

For the salvation of the world it is essential for both those who believe in heaven and those who do not to unite at least in the business of recognizing the common natural values, and of rejecting both the old materialism that ignored the values of matter, and the spirituality that had deviated into Manichaean idealism and betrayed the world for the world beyond, as though it did not have to be prepared for in and through this world.

"I bless you, matter," sang Teilhard, "and you I acclaim: not as the pontiffs of science or the moralizing preachers depict you, debased, disfigured—a mass of brute forces and base appetites—but as you reveal yourself to me today, *in your totality and your true nature.* . . . Sometimes, thinking they are responding to your irresistible appeal, men will hurl themselves for love of you into the exterior abyss of selfish pleasure-seeking: they are deceived by a reflection or by an echo.

"This I now understand.

"If we are ever to reach you, matter, we must, having first established contact with the totality of all that lives and moves here below, come little by little to feel that the individual shapes of all we have laid hold on are melting away in our hands, until finally we are at grips with the *single essence* of all subsistencies and all unions."

This will not come about without a difficult asceticism, however. "Without you, without your onslaughts, without your uprootings of us, we should remain all our lives inert, stagnant; puerile, ignorant both of ourselves and of God. You who batter us and then dress our wounds, you who resist us and yield to us, you who wreck and build, you who shackle and liberate. . . . If we are ever to possess you, having taken you rapturously in our arms, we must then go on to sublimate you through sorrow.

Your realm comprises those serene heights where saints think to avoid you—but where your flesh is so transparent and so agile as to be no longer distinguishable from spirit."

It is a mystery, this matter, which nails us to a cross and yet allows us to save ourselves by lifting this cross. But in this mystery our intelligence catches a glimpse of the Christian truth:

"A Being was taking form in the totality of space; a Being with the attractive power of a soul, palpable like a body, vast as the sky; a Being which mingled with things yet remained distinct from them; a Being of a higher order than the substance of things with which it was adorned, yet taking shape within them." And so the last request confronts our destiny: "Raise me up then, matter, to those heights, through struggle and separation and death; raise me up until, at long last, it becomes possible for me in perfect chastity to embrace the universe. . . .

"The man who is filled with an impassioned love of Jesus hidden in the forces which bring increase to the earth, him the earth will lift up, like a mother, in the immensity of her arms, and will enable him to contemplate the face of God. . . . The man who is filled with an impassioned love for Jesus hidden in the forces which bring death to the earth, him the earth will clasp in the immensity of her arms as her strength fails, and with her he will awaken in the bosom of God."

Love, our vocation, is communion with ourselves, with others, with the human task, with God, but there is no communion without sacrifice: "To receive communion as I die is not sufficient," Teilhard prayed. *"Teach me to make a communion of death itself."*